D0699485

GIVEN GIVING

GIVEN GIVING
Selected Poems of Michel Deguy

Translated by Clayton Eshleman
With an Introduction by Kenneth Koch

UNIVERSITY OF CALIFORNIA PRESS
Berkeley   Los Angeles   London

UNIVERSITY OF CALIFORNIA PRESS
Berkeley and Los Angeles, California

UNIVERSITY OF CALIFORNIA PRESS, LTD.
London, England

Copyright © 1984 by The Regents of the University of California

Library of Congress Cataloging in Publication Data

Deguy, Michel.
  Given giving.

  English and French.
  1. Deguy, Michel—Translations, English.   I. Eshleman, Clayton.
II. Title.
PQ2664.E45A23   1984   841'.914   84–40332
ISBN 0–520–04728–1

Printed in the United States of America

1   2   3   4   5   6   7   8   9

Acknowledgments

Some of these translations have appeared in *Bachy, Bluefish, Coherence, Sulfur,* and *Text,* as well as *The Random House Book of Twentieth-century French Poetry,* edited by Paul Auster. "Histories of Relapses" was published as a Pidgin Press book by Spencer Cholmar.

My gratitude to Michel Deguy himself, with whose help I made a first draft of these translations; to Eric Gans who read the third draft; especially to Bernard Bador who read the penultimate draft and made many helpful suggestions; and to Kenneth Koch who commented on the final draft.

September 1983   C. E.

Table des matières

Contents

Introduction

I first read Michel Deguy's poems in Paris in 1969. I asked Eugene Guillevic, whom I had met in New York, what younger French poets I should read. "Deguy," he said, and I got a copy of *Ouï dire*. I read the poem that begins:

> Vous serez étonnéés d'entendre la liberté de Paul
> Corinthiens II; 11, 19–33, 12, 1–9

I was interested, by its prosiness, its starting seemingly from nowhere, its slightly rough but hesitant music:

> N'gao sud-ouest où dorment les maîtresses
> Parmi le grain que couvent les grains
> Luther et les bardes N'zakara
> Tombes d'accord sur la cuisine[1]

---

[1]You will be astonished to hear the freedom of Paul
Corinthians II: 11, 19–33; 12, 1–9

> (N'gao southwest where the mistresses sleep
> Among grain which is hatched by the grain
> Luther and the N'zakara bards
> Fall into agreement on cuisine)

It was something I hadn't seen before in French poetry.

The French poetry I knew best was the poetry in the great avant-garde tradition from Baudelaire and Rimbaud up through René Char. Despite its enormous variety, there were, in this poetry, certain similarities in tone and theme. Deguy's poems seemed obviously connected to this tradition, but just as obviously to break with it. His subjects; the roughness and prosiness of his music; the inclusion of odd words, rare, scientific, foreign, even of numerals; the changes in tone; the air of being unfinished and unresolved—all this gave a new kind of pleasure and suggested a somewhat different assumption about poetry. For all the differences, the poetry of Rimbaud, Eluard, Reverdy, and others had in common an inclination toward the irrational and the unconscious, away from reasoning and ordinary observation and toward dreams, visions, and strong sensations. Rimbaud believed the real truth was hidden in such places, as did Breton, and that this truth, if poetry could find it, could change the world. Other poets may simply have found the belief in, or search for, such a truth the best way to write poems. Intellect and rationality seemed no help, and in fact, they seemed impediments. Dreams, hallucinations, desires, and so on, were a way to escape them, as was writing, if not "automatically," at least with a very limited conscious control over what one was saying. It is as though poetry were thought of as a separate power, which, aided by such procedures, could go beyond any possible trajectory of intellect. Other ways of getting at the truth—intellectual ones, such as psychology, linguistics, and history—could only be thought of as mistaken paths. The tone of this poetry often has something in common with the tone of revelation—lyrical, often passionate, unified, uninterrupted; the tone of someone who has found out a secret truth, *the* truth—the truth of embracing the summer dawn (Rimbaud), of experiencing the light and shadow on a street (Reverdy).

Deguy's work doesn't show the same confidence in the world of dreams, sensation, and the unconscious. He is interested in how his predecessors wrote—unexpected transitions, confidence in momentary sensations, willingness to remain unclear—but not in their conclusions. The unconscious, the irrational, isn't the answer.

The intellect or, perhaps more precisely, intellectual disciplines, such as psychology and linguistics, come back in his poetry. They come back as directions and as points of view and, verbally, as part of the very texture of Deguy's poems. They are not, however, any more than are dreams and the unconscious, the Answer; in fact, for all their intellectual atmosphere, Deguy's poems suggest that, for him, if anything is the answer it is the happy—or distressing—confusing mixture of all the complicated thoughts and points of view that delineate his subjects. This kind of complexity is expressed not by a sustained lyric tone—this is less revelation than questioning—but by a changing surface of tones, and kinds of language. The poem proceeds, verbally as well as thematically, by means of hesitations, interruptions, changes. It stops, it diverges; it often has an air of being unfinished—even, one could say, of having gone nowhere, the way a moment goes nowhere, a moment of perception or sensation with all its intermixture of memories, associations, ideas.

Deguy's poems seem, for the most part, to be suggested, or inspired, not by general themes or by dreams and hallucinations but by certain kinds of quickly-passing and quickly-caught moments of consciousness. The moments are most often ordinary and unspecial. Their significance is felt but not explained. In "Quadratures/5 p.m.," for example, the soft, cool springtime indoor-outdoor emptiness—with, in the kitchen, the shells being taken off time—is memorable without one's knowing why it was this particular moment that suggested that "the face of things could have been changed."

Deguy of course isn't alone in writing a new, nonsurrealist kind of poetry, though he is an unusual practitioner of it. After World War II, the inspirational force of surrealism seemed just about over. The urgency of recent events—Hitler, the war, the Occupation—probably had something to do with it. Also it is possible that the work begun by Baudelaire and Rimbaud had largely been accomplished. So many brilliant poets had written, so many versions of that magic had been dreamed and expressed. Styles and directions in art don't last forever. Reading Perse and Eluard might inspire more emulation or might incite young poets to do something new.

One can guess what might have seemed wrong, in the 1950s, with that poetry: its leaving out so much, its idealizing, its blurriness, its seeming enclosed, too special, too ecstatic, too sure of its own rhetorical powers. The unconscious, which seemed, and was, such a grand escape from unreality, boredom, and sameness, could end up being a cause of them. In any case, whatever happened, it was true that in the 1950s and 1960s, reading Kant or traveling in South America, for example, could be part of what one wanted to get into a poem. Intellectual details, and also very specifically concrete physical details, became attractive, in the poems of Char, Follain, Guillevic, for example. Words, the nature of words, classes of words, language became a poetic subject also—as in Ponge. There was, too, related to this, a self-consciousness about poetry, a wondering about what it was, if there was anything real about it, if it was worth writing. If poetry wasn't "real," as real as "things," it had no business existing. Some poets renounced poetry. Others were attracted to a sort of poetic minimalism, very few words on mostly blank pages. Deguy seemed to come out of all this undiscouraged, full of energy and ideas, seemingly fascinated by a great variety of experiences— intellectual, emotional, and literary—and liking to get them all into his poems. Rather than choosing one strand, or line, of poetic subject matter and style, as have some of his talented contemporaries (Du Bouchet and Bonnefoy, for example), Deguy seems to me to stay in the center, as if he were unwilling to miss anything, didn't want to give anything up, not any of life or any of the "old privileges" of the poet: being able to rhyme, to tell stories, to write long poems, to mix poetry and prose, to be precise and intellectual, to be ecstatic and lyrical, to write about anything he wants.

He writes about a number of "subjects." That is, his poems begin with a number of different apparent subjects—the most frequent are landscape, woman (unfamiliar, seen in public), woman (known and loved), a place encountered while traveling, a philosophical problem, a text, some aspect of writing poetry. The inspiration is characteristically sudden—a thought coming to mind, a landscape seen for a moment—

Hêtre ou tremble au souffle de femme embrassée[2]

[2]Beech or aspen in the breath of a woman embraced

("Quadratures," from which this line is taken, consists of seven short poems, each inspired by the same place at different hours of a day.) These inspirations (or little shocks, or excitements) seem to start the music, which at once becomes involved with, and is composed of, all sorts of experiential and intellectual associations. If the starting subject is a thought, an attempt at definition, as in "Desire"—

> If desire is that which makes one leave all the rest for the utterly different which is so only in that it is not the rest that one prefers however

the thinking is likely to quickly encounter physical details that make one forget, almost or partly, what is being said—

> estrus, prompt puberty of sweaters, cramps of pines in July. . . .

Poems starting with physical details—

> Hold this moment where she sits down
> Moderating the skirt to the right to the left the eyes
> Her legs drifting on the tiles allowing

are complicated by reflection and by other ways of observing—

> The fingers to find themselves again the pronomial body
>
> On the axis where we—for we *are* on the axis
> Customary sojourn under oblong skies
> Surrounded by earth. . . .

The real subject is where the initial subject has been taken, what the whole poem ends up being, and that seems to be usually, in Deguy's work, an emotional event depicted with intellectual lines. The poems are a sort of "advanced study"—using advanced knowledge and techniques—of momentary states, studies that, as in the poem amusingly titled "Advanced Study" (inspired by a brief stay at Princeton), don't lead to intellectual understanding but to something more immediate and more inclusive, emotionally more the truth. In "Advanced Study" the run to the train station with a woman, with its references to Homeric chariot races, the Annunciation, guillotines, and with its pun on *nom* (*name, noun*) and its bizarre words like *siamoisa* and *comparants* (all suggestive of the

intellectual skills of a scholar) leads to the poet's saying not only that it wasn't he who just ran to the station but that he doesn't even know who it was and, finally, that he has "forgotten what is (going) to begin." He questions his identity and is confused about time. This far-from-clear conclusion of course makes sense artistically and emotionally. These are just the effects a sudden, unexpected intimacy is likely to have.

Deguy writes in a variety of poetic forms, which include various kinds of "prose poems"—the concentrated intellectual prose of "Desire," the broken-up-into-segments prose of "Etc." In this prose poetry there is a characteristic mixture of plain talk, intellectual talk, poetical talk, excited exclamations, and expressions of feeling. Deguy's prose—

> A toast by Cassiopeia herself and Deneb in honor of our last twinklings! The earth in a mantilla of telstars plays Russian roulette, a "call-girl" cassandra on a Concord toward Caracas or Qatar drinks a glass of champagne between the salvos of Orion and Boötes—

is sometimes more "poetic" (in the sense of extravagant and fanciful) than his verse—

> Vous serez étonnées d'entendre la liberté de Paul
> Corinthiens II. . . .

The verse poems are of various lengths. None rhymes in a regular way, though rhyme, like other poetic devices, may every once in a while appear, at the ends of lines—

> Remonte vers l'actrice de nuit cernée Véga
> Comme Yvette Guilbert ou les cils d'un Degas[3]

or elsewhere—

> N'gao sud-ouest où dorment les maîtresses. . . .

Line lengths may be similar or varied; sometimes there are stanzas.

There is, in many of the verse poems, a particular, delicate kind of music that comes less from rhymes, stanzas, and line lengths than from syntax and sense, a music of hesitation, of interruption, of

[3]Reascends toward the night actress eye-ringed Vega
Like Yvette Guilbert or the eyelashes of a Degas

sudden silence. This music seems the result of the lines not being finished, logically or grammatically, and of one line not following the line before it. Often the sense of a line is picked up by the next, but not where the other line left it—from someplace else. Sometimes a line, such as the one about petrels and gannets in "This lady and her beautiful window," is as if abandoned or afloat in the middle of a poem to which it seemingly has no connection. The distance between one line and another may be great, as in this case, or it may be small. In any event, one can't read the poem straight through, as one utterance, in one breath, but must keep pausing. The similarity, or harmony, of sounds from one line to the next, however, draws one on—

> Sa beauté la surface
> L'idolâtrie de nos regards croisés
> Mais de plus près la sueur de son nom perle
> Pourtant "quelle heure est-il"
> Alors j'adopte ses caries
> Plus près plus près
> Le visage s'enfuit en rasant ses terres[4]

One can't say if the prosody creates the content or the content the prosody; probably something of both. The hesitation, the blanks, the slight vagueness indicate the distance from which, and the kind of space in which, the feeling is taking place.

The formal variety of Deguy's poetry (prose poems, verse poems, great variety of both) seems part of his concern with, his fascination with, the nature of poetry. If poetry's relation to the rest of reality is a problem, the solution to it is at least as much in how, as in what, one writes—different forms are different answers, different views of the problem. Poetry and the poet are also subjects he writes about directly. Letting his concern with poetry (what it is, how to make it, what is its purpose) show in his poems is part

[4]Her beauty the surface
The idolatry of our crossed gazes
But closer the sweat of her name beads
Nevertheless "what time is it"
Then I adopt her cavities
Closer   closer
My face takes off razing her lands

of their general openness and inclusiveness, of their tendency to let in and deal with everything that is there.

I have been writing about Deguy's poems as if they were more of a unity than in fact they are. They were written over a period of almost thirty years, and naturally there are changes. A reader going through this book chronologically will see them. Some of the main changes in the verse poems can be seen in reading, say, "The Gulf" and the poem beginning "This lady and her beautiful window." The early, rather Perse-like "The Gulf" is less "intellectual," more openly personal and lyrical, and has a continuing rather than a hesitating, interrupted kind of music. It doesn't change in point of view. It expresses two main feelings—an ecstatic sort of oneness with nature—

> I live at the level of shrill grasshopper bursts.
> And among paper insects scattered by the wind.

and a feeling of difference from nature and of separation from it—

> Everything in me responds to the wind—except . . .
> . . . the voice astonished at its dissimilarity!

Its narrative line is chronological, and it follows its subject to the end. In "This lady and her beautiful window," published six years later (in *Ouï dire*), the hesitating, interrupted music has appeared—

> Cette dame et sa belle fenêtre
> Un ange asymétrique aux ailes porte-vent

There is more variation of tone—

> disait je vous salue
> L'amour distinguait l'absence et la mort

There is language used in a more complicated way—

> Que béatrice soit aussi celle sur qui le temps
> touche un cheveu[5]

---

[5]This lady and her beautiful window
An asymmetrical angel with wind-bearing wings

was saying I greet you
Love distinguished absence and death

May Beatrice also be the one time touches a hair of

(*béatrice* having the sense of *blessèd*—*béate*—and *Beatrice*—Dante's). There are reversals of roles and ambiguity of pronouns (the angel greets Mary; the poet discovers the woman, but it is she who gives him *salut*—greetings, salvation); more daring transitions, greater spaces between things—as in the leap to the last line. Or one could call this last, and much else that is in the poem, change of perspective. The feeling here in regard to nature is not separation, as in "The Gulf," but oneness, at least for a moment, a feeling of union won out of chaos (mêlée) by means of love. The poet and his real (imaginary—idealized) woman are one, in their moment of meeting, with the Angel and Mary in theirs. Each moment is full of the future (a child) and of each future it takes a long time to recognize the meaning. Each of these moments is like the sweet slow meeting of two rivers, the Loire and the Loir (one feminine and one masculine).

The later poem is more sophisticated and intellectual than "The Gulf" but at the same time quite lyric and serene. The complicatedness, the changes of perspective, and the interrupted, hesitating music seem to have helped create a new and interesting artistic balance. In some poems after *Ouï dire* (especially in *Donnant Donnant*), there is somewhat more crowdedness, rush, and momentary intensity, with a correspondingly slightly rough, hurried music (a kind of texture that earlier appeared more often in his prose poems)—

Fais comme si tu m'aimais Montre toi montre moi
Tes Dombes ton Rhine tes Seine ton Ombrie[6]

and, in some poems, published in periodicals since then, a particularly tough sort of intensity applied to physical depiction—

s'encadre sur la porte verte rajustant blonde
a l'électricité la tresse l'onde
et d'une manche glabre de pull
tire sur la jupe au niveau de l'iliaque

Certain characteristics persist, with variations, in Deguy's poetry. There is crowding and hurry, a feeling of richness and rush in the early poems—

[6]Act as if you loved me Show yourself show me
Your Dombes your Rhine your Seine your Umbria

Orienter insistant courber repassant diriger rassembler
dans son souffle incliner joindre[7]

("Le golfe")

though of a simpler kind than, say, in such poems as "Etc.," "Sleeping Under the Star 'N'," "Quadratures," or "I Call Muse"—

Ting tint Orée Auray tent forest stentor Aretino Parrot Tyndareus
Paindoré Tintoretto

("I Call Muse")

vessel that collects urine, oval lucarne of the sky, double-quick
umbrella where the neckties unfold, the male fan, the obscene postcards
born to the sleeve, the map on the table over which the masters stoop,
the antidosis over the grant holder pit, toris exchanged on ring fingers,
pink vestiges from hats. . . .

("Quadratures")

There is a direct, expressive tone—in the late poems likely to
be more complicated and allusive—that persists, too—

The cries of a gull my kisses
That swoop onto the silence of your cheek

("She," in
Fragment du cadastre)

I cannot even without your backbone without your antenna
Tell the time without the clepsydra of your blood

("Iaculatio Tardiva,"
in *Donnant Donnant*)

Always present in Deguy's work are his wit, his experimentation,
his sensuous intellectuality, the seeming urgency of what he has to
say about what moves him to write.

Deguy, though in some of his work he shares a certain adventurous disjunctiveness with some modern American poets, seems
to me more fundamentally lyrical and intent on his own experiences,
say, than Pound; more attached to "making sense" than John
Ashbery; and in general very attached to the French tradition he is
continuing and changing. Writers who seem to have influenced him

[7]To orient insistent to curve coming back lead gather in its
blowing to bend to join

include, for the early work, Eluard and Perse, and for the later, Mallarmé and Jouve.

Poetry is hard to translate. Deguy's, which, like Mallarmé's, for example, is very much embedded in French words and usages, is especially so. Clayton Eshleman, I think, has done exactly the right thing in aiming to be completely accurate and at the same time to give the reader an experience in English equivalent to what he'd have reading Deguy in French.

Kenneth Koch

de *Fragment du cadastre*
from *Fragment of the Cadastre*

Le golfe

Le long été commence où croît et décroît l'ambition.
Je vis au niveau des éruptions stridentes des sauterelles.
Et parmi les insectes de papier que disperse le vent.
Il y a du seigle sur les genoux de l'écrivain et dans son dos pleuvent
    les blés.
L'oreille appliquée à la terre entend son sang.
Il est le désœuvré.

La roue du paysage tourne sous le triomphe du soleil.
Les raies blanches du ciel convergent au-delà de la terre
Les îles s'effilochent, la marée décèle des ruches d'algues couleurs de
    débris
Où fermentent des invertébrés.
Vois toute la rotation horizontale du golfe,
Le glissement des bocages, le grincement des bornages de genêt,
Rayons verts sur le moyeu de l'horizon!

Si je reprends les chemins profonds—faut-il encore s'en entretenir?
Je vais lentement aux rendez-vous essentiels
Le vent traverse la presqu'île pliant les blés vers l'Est.
Partout la mer m'assaille car le vent du large lui ouvre passage entre
    les haies
Entre les orges entre les châtaigniers
L'Océan épais monte entre les toits.

Le vent rapide descend les trois hauts degrés des pins, des genêts et
    des blés;
Il se rue frôlant les oreilles et passe.
Le soleil à reculons fait face. Le soleil acrobate descend du chapiteau,
Interminable.
Parfois des spectateurs repèrent l'exercice. Mais beaucoup l'été se
    couchent avant la fin.

Le vent parle trop fort

The Gulf

The long summer begins where ambition grows and declines.
I live at the level of shrill grasshopper bursts.
And among paper insects scattered by the wind.
There is rye on the writer's knees, wheat rains down on his back.
His ear pressed to the ground hears his blood.
He is the idle one.

The wheel of the landscape turns under the triumph of the sun.
The white bands of the sky converge beyond the earth
Islands fray, the tide divulges beehives of debris-colored algae
Where invertebrates ferment.
See all of the horizontal rotation of the gulf,
The glide of copses, the creak of broom demarcations,
Green spokes on the horizon's hub!

If I return on the sunken paths—need it be mentioned again?
I slowly wander to the essential meetings
The wind crosses the peninsula bending the wheat eastward.
On every side the sea assails me for the open sea wind forces a passage
      for it through the hedges
Through the barley through the chestnut trees
Solid ocean rises between the roofs.

The wind rapidly descends the three steep steps of pines, broom and
      wheat;
It rushes brushing my ears and is gone.
The sun, facing backwards. The acrobat sun descends the capital,
Interminable.
Sometimes spectators notice the exercises. But many during the
      summer retire before they are completed.

The wind speaks too loud
Into its holes sneak dogs from distant farms.
The lark keeps falling. The wind tunnels into the fields' front ranks.

Dans les trous du vent se glissent les chiens des fermes éloignées.
L'alouette ne cesse de tomber. Le vent se fraie un passage jusqu'aux
    premiers rangs des champs.
Il enjambe violemment la lisière de paille et se jette aux oreilles.

Des chiens gardent des chemins sans importance d'où je suis.
Les voix qui miment les bêtes pour leur commander,
Issues des niches plus hautes où elles veillent sur les biens,
Passent par les trous du vent
Hélant pour des travaux sans importance d'où je suis.

Promenades en vue de quoi?
Le corbeau sans couleur,
La mouette qui arrête le vent,
La lune, cirrus obèse, qui marque où le vent ne souffle plus.

Car il manque aux pas la constance du vent
Du vent qui sait aux papillons aux fougères aux nuages
Indiquer la direction
Orienter insistant courber repassant diriger rassembler dans son
    souffle incliner joindre
—et tout à coup redresser cabrer recourber tordre;
Le vent parcourt le site, ajointe et fait communiquer les lignes du site;
Lui de haut de partout les suit;
C'est lui qui trace les sillons du site.

Tout en moi répond au vent—sauf. . .
Tout plie sous l'injonction qui assemble:
les cheveux comme un champ plus dense
le dos pareil aux troncs, les yeux dessillés sous le sel
les jambes écroulées dans les pierres
Et la manducation au bruit de charrette; tout. . .
Sauf la voix debout qui demande où elle naît; tout
Sauf la voix étonnée de sa dissemblance!

Le grand vaisseau du matin appareille:
Cris de poulies des mouettes; cordages du soleil dans les yeux;

It steps violently over the straw boundary and hurls itself at one's
    ears.

Dogs guard paths that are unimportant from where I am.
Voices that imitate cattle so to control them
Issue from higher niches where they keep watch on property,
They pass through the holes of the wind
Hollering to work unimportant from where I am.

Promenades in view of what?
The colorless crow,
The gull checking the wind,
The moon, obese cirrus, marking where wind no longer blows.

For steps don't have the constancy of the wind
The wind that knows how to indicate the way
For butterflies ferns and clouds
To orient insistent to curve coming back lead gather in its blowing to
    bend to join
—suddenly to lift rear curve back twist;
The wind sweeps over the site, conjoins and links the site's lines;
Follows it from above everywhere;
It is the wind that traces the site's furrows.

Everything in me responds to the wind—except . . .
Everything bends to the injunction that assembles:
The hair like an even denser field
The back like trunks, the eyes unsealed under the salt
The legs crumbled among stones
And the manducation like the noise of a cart; everything . . .
Except the erect voice that asks where was it born; everything
Except the voice astonished at its dissimilarity!

The great vessel of morning sets sail:
Pulley cries of gulls; sun cordage in one's eyes; lofty staysails of
    cumuli hoisted folded driven; a crew of larks swooping over the
    ash trees' lower yards; the crow quartermasters

hautes trinquettes des cumulus hissées brassées drossées; un équipage d'alouettes qui survole les basses vergues des frênes; les corbeaux quartiers-maîtres

Et le grand spinaker de l'orage. . .

Du Morbihan.

And the great spinnaker of the storm . . .

Morbihan

Le cimetière

Enclos d'un mur bas de pierres inégales et que l'âge enfonce dans les
    scabieuses,
Porté au ciel aux quatre coins par le jet noir de plantes arborescentes :
Trajectoires de scories figées, colonnes d'encre aux franges de
    mimosa,
Les cyprès filtres du chant le plus anxieux des vents.

Qui laboure la terre consacrée ?
Qui change en dalles les rectangles d'herbe,
Et reprend chaque jour aux fleurs la surface d'un homme ?
Qui jadis a circonscrit près des villages l'aire assignée
    au recel des morts ?
Qui aboie quand le chien invisible aboie ?
Et là-bas, la meule d'azur aiguise les faîtes
Et l'ardoise effilée brille.

De Tumiac.

The Cemetery

Enclosed by a low wall of odd-shaped stones which age sinks into the
   scabious,
At each corner lifted to the sky by the black jets of arborescent
   plants:
Trajectories of frozen slag, columns of ink with mimosa fringes,
The cypresses filters of the wind's most edgy song.

Who plows these hallowed grounds?
Who changes the grass rectangles into slabs,
And every day takes back a human surface from the flowers?
Who long ago near the villages circumscribed the assigned area for
   pawning the dead?
Who barks when the invisible dog barks?
Beyond, the azure grindstone sharpens the roof ridges
And the tapered slate glistens.

Tumiac

La blanchisserie

Le vent déchire les étangs
La lune les reprise avec un fil de verre
Vieille chauve à la mansarde des nuages
Elle coud la ravaudeuse

Quand tout le monde est endormi
Elle descend de sa lucarne
Je la vois mettre aux champs de grandes pièces grises

Seule
Elle sort toute la lingerie
Elle accroche aux saules humides
La dentelle des brumes
Et tend d'une colline à l'autre
Les chaussettes des sentiers

Elle amidonne les névés
Défripe la crinoline des mers
Dans les ports elle glace les voiles
La repasseuse
Et lisse les grands pans d'ardoise

Je la vois qui s'active
La blanchisseuse
Et bientôt l'aube vient ternir
Les habits de lumière

De Tumiac.

The Laundry

The wind shreds the ponds
The moon mends them with a glass thread
Old bald woman in her mansard of clouds
She sews, the darner

When everyone is asleep
She descends from her lucarne
I see her putting huge grey patches on the fields

Alone
She takes out the lingerie
Hangs on humid willows
The lace of mist
And from one hill to another stretches
The stockings of the paths

She starches the firns
Smoothes out the crinoline of the seas
In the ports she freezes the sails
The ironer
And finishes the great slate surfaces

I see her bustling about
The laundry woman
Soon dawn will tarnish
The spangled garb

Tumiac

Elle

A l'aube de ton cou horizontal
Les cris de mouette mes baisers
Qui s'abattent sur le silence de ta joue
—battement de mes bouches plaintives
Vol au port de tes yeux
Qui se laissent piller comme l'eau taciturne—
Et rentrent nidifier
Dans la saison des cheveux persistants.

2

Maintenant cet énorme visage qui cache le monde
Ces cheveux comme une Beauce d'été
La falaise du front et la bouche autonome
Lèvres deux bêtes se caressent flanc à flanc
L'œil oiseau mordoré qui mime son envol
Et les beaux galets des genoux
Le cou gerbe de sang le jeune bouleau tiède

> Pas un mot du soliloque
> Qui vaille de laisser
> Le faisceau blanc des os

3

Lui chargé de mourir
Hébété sous l'armure puérile
Il revient boire une dernière fois
Au bol de thé de ses cheveux

Elle
L'enrôlée muette au défilé pangynique
La sexuelle

She

1

At the dawn of your horizontal neck
The cries of a gull my kisses
That swoop onto the silence of your cheek
—beating of my plaintive mouths'
Flight to the port of your eyes
Open to pillage like taciturn water—
And return to nest
In the season of nondeciduous hair.

2

Now this enormous face that hides the world
This hair like a Beauce in summer
The cliff of the forehead and the autonomous mouth
Lips two animals that caress each other flank to flank
The eye a bronzed bird that mimes its ascent
And the lovely pebbles of knees
The neck a sheaf of blood the warm young birch

> Not a word of the soliloquy
> Justifies leaving
> The white stack of bones

3

He, charged with dying
Dumbstruck beneath the puerile armor
He returns to drink for the last time
From the bowl of tea of her hair

She
Mutely drawn in to the pangynic parade
The sexual one

Parmi les provocatrices des villes
Battant le pavillon des seins
Sur la hampe cambrée qui pose au fourreau noir
Elles
Les revendicatrices

4

Elle
présence de la présence
Elle qui devrait simplement être là
Epiphanie de l'apparition
figure de naissance
et son accueil couler de source,
Elle
qui devrait donner à voir
la présence
Pour que les choses aient lieu
En sa présence

Among the seductresses of the cities
Flying the colors of breasts
From the arched pole that poses as a black sheath
They
The revindicatresses

4

    She
    presence of the presence
    She who should simply be there
    Epiphany of the apparition
    figure of birth
    and her welcome flows freely,
    She
    who should allow presence
    to be seen
    So that things might occur
    In her presence

de *Poèmes de la presqu'île*
from *Poems on the Peninsula*

Seuil

Le soir quand j'entre dans la forêt de mon sommeil, lunettes d'ombre aux yeux chargés, écartant des buissons de lueurs, par d'obscurs sentiers cheminant vers la source des larmes, les faisceaux de la nuit me précèdent. Ce qui persiste du jour s'avance vers les yeux immobiles.

Nuit giboyeuse, ne sait-elle pas lier les mains du poème? Et je voudrais t'aimer deviendrait je t'aime. . .

Mais veille plutôt! car la terre est le grand vestige.

Défouis l'origine qu'elle garde, la grande trace où l'absence se fige. L'espérance confie que t'attend un pays dont cet amour d'écrire est l'acte de naissance.

Threshold

At night when I enter the forest of my sleep, shadow glasses with loaded eyes, parting thickets of gleams, traveling along obscure paths toward the source of tears, the beams of the night precede me. What persists of the day advances toward the unmoving eyes.

The game-filled night, doesn't it know how to tie the poem's hands? And I would like to love you would become I love you . . .

But rather keep alert! for earth is the great vestige.

Unbury the origin that it guards, the wide trail where absence congeals. The hope confides that you are awaited by a country whose love of writing is the act of birth.

O la grande apposition du monde

un champ de roses près d'un
champ de blé et deux enfants rouges dans le champ voisin du champ
de roses et un champ de maïs près du champ de blé et deux saules
vieux à la jointure; le chant de deux enfants roses dans le champ de
blé près du champ de roses et deux vieux saules qui veillent les roses
les blés les enfants rouges et le maïs

Le bleu boit comme tache
L'encre blanche des nuages
Les enfants sont aussi mon
Chemin de campagne

O great apposition of the world

                                a rose field near a wheat field and
two red children in the field bordering on the rose field and a corn
field near the wheat field and two old willows where they join; the
song of two rose children in the wheat field near the rose field and
two old willows keeping watch over the roses the wheat the red
children and the corn

        The blue blots like a spot
        The white ink of clouds
        Children are also my
        Country path

Le traître

Les grands vents féodaux courrent la terre.

Poursuite pure ils couchent les blés, délitent les fleuves, effeuillent chaume et ardoises, seigneurs, et le peuple des hommes leur tend des pièges de tremble, érige des pals de cyprès, jette des grilles de bambou en travers de leurs pistes, et leur opposent de hautes éoliennes.

Le poète est le traître qui ravitaille l'autan, il rythme sa course et la presse avec ses lyres, lui montre des passages de lisière et de cols.

The Traitor

Great feudal winds rush about the earth.

Pure pursuit they lay low the wheat, surbed the rivers, shed thatch and slate, lords, and the people of men put out aspen traps for them, erect cypress stakes, throw bamboo railings across their paths, and oppose them with tall windmills.

The poet is the traitor who provides supplies to the southwind, he rhythms its course and urges it on with his lyres, points out passages in the forest's edge and in the cols.

Le pommier

J'ai attendu, comme un amant aux champs prend rendez-vous sous le pommier rigide, et dans l'herbe qui jaunit attend tout l'après-midi sous des tonnes de nuages. L'amante ne vient pas.

Ce qui est rien, peut-il être cerné—margelle des poignets tordus, tresse des yeux de plusieurs en rond, spirale des croassements qui défoncent; anneau de voix; mon mal, mon mal, transcendance qui irrompt, jetant à terre ici le fourbu geignant de cette déposition, Ulysse rustique (il chasse les poules ataxiques) aux yeux charnus, du vent plein la face, l'évanoui qui ne cesse «où suis-je?». Mémoire du don des choses prudentes qui tâtonnent sur la mince couche de glace du monde.

Sous un pommier charmant, étendu mais trop bavard pour le poème (pourtant la marée grimpe dans les branches basses cherchant un nid dans l'abri vert), est-ce notre lot de ne plus avoir à songer que des conflits d'hommes?

The Apple Tree

I have waited, like a lover in the fields makes a date under the tense apple tree, and in the yellowing grass waits all afternoon under tons of clouds. The loved one does not come.

What is nothing, can it be surrounded—curbstone of twisted wrists, plait of eyes of several in a circle, spiral of cawings that break through; ring of voices; my sickness, my sickness, a transcendence that erupts, flinging to the ground here the foundered one complaining about this deposition, rustic Ulysses (he shoos away the ataxic hens) with fleshy eyes, a face full of wind, the swooner who doesn't cease "where am I?" Memory of the gift of prudent things that walk gingerly across the thin layer of ice of the world.

Under the lovely apple tree, stretched out but too talkative for the poem (however the tide climbs the low branches looking for a nest in the green shelter), is it our lot to have nothing to daydream about except human conflict?

Roi soleil

Quand le roi se levait de bonne heure
Marchait au fond dans l'eau du matin

Le scaphandre aux souliers de soie
Longe les combles poissonneux
Hante les palais démâtés
Dans l'aube dorée sans courant
Luit un banc d'ardoises squameuses

La vase et l'épave le roi rêve
De les quitter si haut qu'il connaisse
A l'autre bord du jour transparent
Le pêcheur rouge penché qui verse
Au fond ses hameçons de lumière

Sun King

When the king would rise early
He would walk the bottom of morning's pool

The diving suit in silk shoes
Skirts the fish-filled garret
Haunts the dismasted palaces
In the gilded currentless dawn
A shoal of scaly slates gleams

The slime and the wreckage the king dreams
Of leaving them so high that he will know
On the far shore of the transparent day
The red bent fisherman spilling
Into the depths his fishhooks of light

Le miroir

Ville aveuglée à moins que ne la montre
A soi une rivière
Elle tire partage de l'eau
Et s'assied chez soi sur les berges
Un côté garde l'autre ils s'opposent et se voient
La rive se reflète en l'autre
Et chacune soi-même en le fleuve
Lui la dédouble et ainsi la redouble
Et permet qu'elle se connaisse

The Mirror

Town blinded unless shown
To itself by a river
It draws its share from the water
And sits at home on the banks
One side takes care of the other they oppose and see each other
One bank is reflected in the other
And each itself in the river
Which undoubles it and in that way redoubles it
Allowing it to know itself

Les yeux

Cri de corbeau des yeux qu'enfoncent les poings en deuil:
Le même bruit sous les paupières closes, où le même hiver pâle attend
Tes yeux longeaient mes yeux; ils rampaient jus-qu'aux miens
Cherchant la mire invisible où j'eusse aimé paraître Puis tes yeux se cabraient
La bête agile des prunelles, toute la violence de l'autre espèce s'y résume; mais les yeux encerclés de mémoire, rapides comme l'oiseau, les yeux sont retenus captifs aux menottes des os
Cri de corbeau le même cri sous les paupières closes où le pâle hiver de mémoire sommeille

The Eyes

Crow cry of eyes that fists in mourning grind into:
The same sound under closed eyelids, where the same pale winter
waits
Your eyes skirted mine; they crawled up to mine
Seeking the invisible aim where I should have loved to appear
Then your eyes were rearing
The agile beast of pupils, all the violence of the other species is
summed up there; but the eyes encircled with memory, quick as a
bird, the eyes are held captive by bone handcuffs
Crow cry the same cry under the closed eyelids where the pale
winter of memory dozes

L'effacement

Ton visage redevient chat; tout se décompose et remonte le millénaire. Tes dents se lèvent comme aube boréale, et ta face un grand décor originel.

De si près—indéchiffrable autant que l'ensemble, un étrange moment durant, évanouie la tardive beauté.

> Lionne à crinière de saule, lionne
> La vie se dissipe.
> Nus sous le grand igloo

Effacement

Your face becomes a cat again; everything decomposes and goes back up the millennium. Your teeth rise like a dawn borealis, and your face a huge primal set.

From so close—indecipherable as the whole thing, during a peculiar moment, vanished the belated beauty.

> Willow-maned lioness, lioness
> Life disperses.
> Nudes under the great igloo

de *Biefs*
from *Millraces*

Chaque fois qu'il fige l'unité de sa vie dans des règles
Chaque fois que des gestes jaloux miment sa foi avec exactitude
Il est ceinturé comme une île d'eau et d'oiseaux troubles

Chaque fois qu'il fixe le temps
La sève l'encercle   Le mal croît dans ses granges
Son fils bientôt le déserte   L'été le désespère
Un principe nouveau déshonore ses filles

Le sage laisserait bien virer le temps comme un éper-
vier sur la cour qu'il nourrit de ses morts Mais
l'imprévisible grandit
Alors il est besoin d'un prophète moqueur

Each time that he fixes the unity of his life into rules
Each time that jealous gestures mime his faith with exactitude
He is surrounded like an island with water and with murky birds

Each time that he fixes time
Sap encircles him   Evil grows in his barns
His son soon deserts him   Summer drives him to despair
A new principle dishonors his daughters

The sage would like to let time gyre like a sparrow hawk
over the courtyard which he nourishes with his dead But
the unforeseeable looms even larger
Then a mocking prophet is needed

EACH TIME THAT HE FIXES   37

Beaucoup de vent affecté à ce lieu
Et le cri des ruminants comme un genévrier fendu par la tempête

Ce lieu me suffit
Où le parfum n'est pas rare
Mais la même senteur d'algue et d'hortensia
Dans les linges fins de l'air

Chaque case d'herbage assemble
Le cheval et la vache en pose animale:
D'attente écartelée   blason de l'ultime
Un œil sur chaque côté du monde
Effroi

Très tôt et très tard comme tout point d'un cercle
Depuis longtemps poète et pas encore, jamais . . .
Plus loin! Nous rapporterons la carte que vous n'avez pas!
Pourtant me suffit ce lieu
Où déjà des hommes simples ameutaient le granit

Dix-huitième heure
La mer étend ses mains diaphanes vers l'épaule veiue des rives
Comme Isaac tâtonnant la toison de Jacob

Lots of wind assigned to this place
And the ruminants' cry like a juniper split by the tempest

This place satisfies me
Where the perfume is not rare
But the same scent of algae and hydrangea
In the fine linen of the air

Each square of herbage assembles
The horse and the cow in an animal pose:
Of quartered waiting   blazon of the ultimate
An eye on each side of the world
Dread

Very soon and very late like every point on a circle
For so long a poet and not yet, never . . .
Further! We will bring the map that you do not have!
Yet it satisfies me this place
Where already simple men are rousing the granite

Eighteenth hour
The sea extends its diaphanous hands toward the shores' hairy
    shoulders
Like Isaac groping Jacob's fleece

Ce bal assez paisible où les arbres ont costume d'arbre et un tapis de terre est jeté sur le centre où les morts mêmes ne peuvent parvenir mangeurs de cailloux et les ongles révulsés contre la porte impraticable et où le voile d'herbes et d'air, de laines et de couleurs et de trompeuse transparence d'eau prend l'homme au corps et jusqu'au masque dur des mâchoires et monte jusqu'aux yeux

seuls

où un peu de nudité parfois tressaille

This rather peaceful ball where the trees are dressed up as trees and a carpet of earth is thrown on the center which even the dead cannot reach pebble-eaters with nails turned up against the impassable door and where the veil of grass and air, of wool and colors and the delusive transparency of water takes a man by the body up to the hard mask of his jaws and rises up to his eyes
                                                                                        alone
         where a little nakedness occasionally trembles

Une tasse sur un télégramme
«Quand rentres-tu»
L'aube comme une trame très fine sur le métier
du soir
«O douceur douceur»
Visage trop nu je recule

Mais prévoyant que la panique a un sens le monde en vrac se rue
sur la place afin qu'avec la simplicité de l'estampe nous élisions
quelques lignes les plus simples pareils aux vanniers qui d'un même
roseau font maintes corbeilles

A cup on a telegram
"When are you coming back"
Dawn like a very fine woof on the loom
of evening
"Oh sweetness sweetness"
Face too naked I retreat

But foreseeing that panic means something the world unbaled rushes
to the plaza so that with the simplicity of an engraving we elect a
few lines the simplest ones like the basket makers who with the
same reed weave many baskets

de *Ouï dire*
from *By Ear*

Le poète de profil
Le poète à l'équerre de corps et d'ombre sur les seuils
Le poète Gulliver qui retrace un roncier d'hiver avec la pointe de
     Hopkins
Ou décroît pour accorder l'herbe au zodiaque avec compas de
     Gongora
Génie des contes perses car il refuse l'indifférence

Il entretient la lymphe bleue dans le réseau des ormes
Veille zêta epsilon delta d'Orion sur la branche basse
Œil triple posé de witch 1 witch 2 witch 3
Qui s'envole constellation subtile de corbeaux

Il est ici pour inventer quelque chose d'aussi beau qu'un mot *saxi-
     frage* inventé par personne
S'il cherche un trésor il le trouve
(Imagine un poisson cherchant un poisson dans l'obscurité des
     mers . . .)

Quand il revient parmi nous dans la transparence d'hiver où les
     choses sont des lignes
Quand il rouvre le filon des couleurs à ciel ouvert
Quand il revient sur l'étroite digue hospitalière et

Victoire fendant le sol figé sachant
Que la vie déserte à quelques mètres de hauteur
Quand il retrouve son totem en boules couleur d'excrément
Dans les petits pommiers français près d'où on range les araires

Et quand poussé aux épaules par
Comme un transféré
Il longe la rivière invitée au moulin
Le coq sa crête de lilas son cri à travers
     —L'aveugle

The poet in profile
The poet at right angle with body and shadow on the thresholds
The poet Gulliver retracing a winter bramble with Hopkins's point
Or diminishing to align the grass with the Zodiac using Gongora's
     compasses
A genie of Persian tales because he refuses indifference

He entertains the blue lymph in a network of elms
Watches over the zeta epsilon delta of Orion on the low branch
Alit triple eye of witch 1 witch 2 witch 3
Which flies off a subtle constellation of crows

He is here to invent something as beautiful as a word *saxifrage*
     invented by no one
If he searches for a treasure he finds it
(Imagine a fish searching for a fish in ocean dark . . .)

When he returns among us in winter transparency where things are
     lines
When he opens the lode of colors out in the open
When he returns to the narrow hospitable dike and

Victory cleaving the hardened soil knowing
That at several meters high life gives up
When again he finds his totem in excrement-colored balls
In the little French apple trees near which the swing ploughs are
     stored

And when pushed on the shoulders by
Like one transferred
He skirts the river invited to the mill
The cock its lilac comb its cry across
     —The blind man
     He puts on willow gloves

Il se gante de saule
Il endosse la rivière
Et voici   tâtonnant
Sa main prolongée
S'avance dans un monde étrange
Il se hâte vers le désert Un plateau où la flèche est gnomon
Le vide est sa force Le soleil passe comme un anneau nuptial
Entre les arbres généreux il appartient à la déception
Émigré que scalpe un âge il travaille pour une absente sous ses pieds
        qui dort quand il se lève
Pour regagner l'absente de son pays qui veille quand il dort
Le temps est celui qu'il n'a pas de penser à elle

Il émigrait l'hiver dans les branches pieuses
L'hiver d'une seule manière multipliée
—les os les mots l'amplitude les pas les voix l'espace occupé les voy-
        ages la justice—
Épiant le visible où les figures muent
Il émigrait faune serrant un pipeau de veines
Syrinx étouffée les vaisseaux creux ramassés devant soi
Où le sang prolonge sa peine Le cœur venait contre l'oreille

On veut le faire roi!
        La clientèle des vents le serre
Les cris le portent
        Toute voix veut à nouveau se faire entendre
L'hiver expose les litiges
Un groupe de fleurs attend son tour
Il y a ces écrouelles de lisière Il y a ces ruines
Un joug un front de buffle brûlé
        Qui t'a fait ruine?

La crase des mains apaise droite et gauche
Une pierre attendit cent mille ans Il exauce le silex
Un jouet d'ébonite sur un sillon quoi d'autre
Car les *adunata* quittant le rêve atterrissent

He dons the river
And here   groping
His hand protracted
Advancing in a strange world
He hastens toward the desert A plateau where the spire is a gnomon
The void is his strength The sun passes like a wedding ring
Between the generous trees he belongs to deceit
An immigrant scalped by an age he works for an absent woman under
      his feet who sleeps when he rises
To recover the absent one of his own country who stays awake when
      he sleeps
Time is that which he does not have to think about her

He emigrated during the winter in the pious branches
The winter of a single multiplied manner
—the bones the words the amplitude the steps the voices the
      occupied space the journeys the justice—
Spying on the visible where figures mutate
He emigrated a faun clutching a vein pipe
Choked Syrinx the vessels hollow gathered before him
Where blood prolongs his pain His heart was pressing against his ear

They want to make him king!
      The clientele of winds press him
Shouts carry him
      Every voice wants to be heard again
Winter explains the litigations
A group of flowers awaits its turn
There is that scrofula of the forest's edge There are those ruins
A yoke a burnt buffalo forehead
      Who made you a ruin?

The crasis of hands appeases right and left
A stone waited a hundred thousand years He answers the flint's
      prayer
An ebonite toy in a furrow what else

Tout le réel est possible
Les fables parlent comme des animaux

Ombre de Virgile devenue voix de Virgile
Voix de muse devenue désir et obéissance
Je te suis   écoutant la plainte donnant voix à
l'enfer fraternel   Je t'écoute   ta voix décapitée
attentif au silence continue sous le treillis pareil au vengeur qui canne
      la vengeance

Je reconnais la souffrance grâce aux lieux
L'herbe ici n'a pas crû La bête est restée
Toi je t'écoute Que dis-tu de ta saison?
Je descends la vallée partageant
                              Une feuille
Remonte vers le village

Les stères d'os rassemblez-les au feu
Le tort? Mais l'homme vous donne la place
Les oiseaux ont des chemins Qu'on relève cette borne
L'eau qu'elle se dessèche en cette place usurpée
      Dénouez les andouillers des acacias lutteurs
         Retirez doucement le bleu cosmos
         Qui s'est pris aux pals d'hiver

Les fleuves   la perspective
Les versants   le fagot des chemins
Il guide vers un lit de syllabes

Le vent est son fouet
Il favorise la transhumance des terres
Appelle bruit le grondement des sols
Longeant l'arc où le ciel
A centré ses lumières
Cyprès de paroles alors
Se dressent et oscillent

For the *adunata*, leaving the dream, land
All the real is possible
Fables speak like animals

Virgil shade become Virgil voice
Muse voice become desire and obedience
I follow you   listening to the plaint giving voice to
The fraternal hell   I listen to you   your decapitated voice
attentive to the silence continuing under the trellis just like the
      avenger plaiting vengeance

I recognize the suffering thanks to the places
The grass here did not grow The animal remained
You I listen to you What are you saying about your season?
I descend the valley sharing
                                        A leaf
Goes back up toward the village

The ricks of bones gather them in the fire
The wrong? But man offers you a place
The birds have paths Let this milestone be lifted
The water let it dry up in this usurped place
      Untie the antlers of struggling acacias
         Gently withdraw the blue cosmos
         Caught on the stakes of winter

The rivers   the perspective
The slopes   the bundled paths
He leads toward a bed of syllables

The wind is his whip
He favors the transhumance of lands
Calls the grumbling soils noise
Walking along the arc where the sky
Has centered its lights
Speech cypresses then
Sand up and sway

Par ceux qui marchent ici comme dans galerie à ciel
        ouvert (parois d'ormes piliers de grès sol de terre
        ciel de ciel) par ceux qui disent
Voici lisière
Le monde avait besoin d'être annoncé
« Le royaume est semblable au chemin par exemple
Extérieur au mur bas du château grillagé
Le royaume est semblable à ce lieu
Qui a besoin de parabole pour demeure. »

By those who walk here as in an open cast
      gallery (walls of elm sandstone pillars earthen earth
      skied sky) by those who say
Here is the forest's edge
The world needed to be proclaimed
"The kingdom is like a path for example
Outside the low wall of the wire-netted chateau
The kingdom is like this place
Which needs a parable as a dwelling."

Un homme las du génitif et las
De l'histoire du même divisé contre lui-même

    —ô femmes répudiées—
Portant les faisceaux du savoir
Mais en forme des faux sur le champ

Apostrophes sur les tempes
Près des bêtes tachées qui mourraient jusqu'au bord

    Le vent repasse
Par des chenaux sans métamorphoses
Un géomètre le soleil reprend les verticales
    Phares lents d'ombre

Quel est ton héritage?
Entre audience et décret le suspens
Royal comme la dot des Phéaciens
L'accueil à mots couverts de ressemblance errante
La vengeance son change en manne
Le remembrement des tropes
Le baptême des noms après les noms

O mer limitée! Ignorance des ronces!
Sous les paupières nous nous rapprochons
Pour parler en secret à son insu à mon insu
Je prends le masque de la terre sous la peau
    L'herbe envahit mes os

A man tired of the genitive and tired
Of the story of the same divided against itself

      —oh repudiated women—
Bearing the bundles of knowing
But in the shape of scythes on the field

Apostrophes on the human temples
Beside the spotted beasts that would die to the edge

      The wind repasses
Through fairways without metamorphoses
A geometer the sun retakes the verticals
      Slow beacons of shade

What is your heritage?
Between audience and decree the suspense
Royal as Phaeacian dowry
The welcome in cryptic speech of errant likeness
The vengeance its exchange in manna
The regrouping of tropes
The baptism of name after name

O limited sea! Ignorance of brambles!
Under our eyelids we get closer to each other
To talk in secret without the other knowing without my knowing
I take the mask of the earth under my skin
      Grass invades my bones

Quand le vent pille le village
Tordant les cris
L'oiseau
S'engouffre dans le soleil

Tout est ruine
Et la ruine
Un contour spirituel

.

When the wind sacks the village
Twisting the cries
The bird
Engulfs itself in the sun

All is ruin
And ruin
A spiritual contour

C'est entre nous
L'air entre les mains salut
Et la main entre les saluts
Et le salut pur intervalle
Rien avec rien jouant à
S'envoyer la belle apparition

It's between us
The air between our hands a greeting
And the hand between the greetings
And the greeting pure interval
Nothing with nothing playing at
Bandying the beautiful apparition

Les jours ne sont pas comptés
Sachons former un convoi de déportés qui chantent
Arbres à flancs de prières
Ophélie au flottage du temps
Assonances guidant un sens vers le lit du poème

Comment appellerons-nous ce qui donne le ton?
La poésie comme l'amour risque tout sur des signes

The days are not numbered
Let's learn how to form a convoy of singing deportees
Trees with flanks of prayer
Ophelia at the floating of time
Assonances guiding a meaning toward the poem's bed

How shall we name what sets the pitch?
Poetry like love risks everything on signs

Alluvion des cris Minerai d'hirondelles
Dans le delta du vent les plissements du vent
    La trembleraie bleuit
Le pouls de l'étang bat
       Toutes les trois heures un poème
       Devient nouveau puis se ternit
       Sous la lecture Recroît dans le silence

Alluvium of cries Ore of swallows
In the delta of wind the foldings of wind
	The aspen grove turns blue
The pond's pulse beats
		Every three hours a poem
		Becomes new then tarnishes
		Under the reading Grows again in the silence

Quai gris d'où tombe l'appât de neige
Le jour décline dans sa coïncidence
L'homme et la femme échangent leur visage
Le vin est lent sur le tableau
A passer dans son sablier de verre
Et l'artiste rapide au cœur par symboles
Doué de confiance hésite:
La pierre est-elle plus belle dans le mur?

Grey pier from where the snow bait falls
The day declines into its coincidence
The man and the woman exchange their faces
The wine is slow on the painting
To pass through its hourglass
And the artist quick to the heart through symbols
Gifted with confidence hesitates:
Is the stone more beautiful in the wall?

Vous serez étonnés d'entendre la liberté de Paul
Corinthiens II; 11, 19–33; 12, 1–9
L'ouïe éduquée depuis naissance au rythme
Entend «ce nom auquel silencieusement je crois»
L'iambe monte et descend dans la maison

(N'gao sud-ouest où dorment les maîtresses
Parmi le grain que couvent les grains
Luther et les bardes N'zakara
Tombent d'accord sur la cuisine)

L'homme en aube dimanche surpassé
Vante une croisade grande comme une chasse à l'homme
Que la croisée Rennes-Raspail enraye

You will be astonished to hear the freedom of Paul
Corinthians II: 11, 19–33; 12, 1–9
One's hearing brought up since birth on rhythm
Hears "this name in which I silently believe"
The iamb rises and falls in the house

(N'gao southwest where the mistresses sleep
Among grain which is hatched by the grain
Luther and the N'zakara bards
Fall into agreement on cuisine)

The man in an alb Sunday surpassed
Extols a crusade big as a man hunt
Which the Rennes-Raspail intersection jams

Moraine bleue dans le glacier du soir

La vigne rentre sous le vert, le bleu reprend le ciel, le sol s'efface dans la terre, le rouge s'exhausse et absorbe en lui les champs de Crau. Les couleurs s'affranchissent des choses et retrouvent leur règne épais et libre avant les choses, pareilles à la glaise qui précédait Adam

Le saurien terre émerge et lève mâchoire vers la lune, les années rêveuses sortent des grottes et rôdent tendrement autour de la peau épaisse Falaise se redresse, Victoire reprend son âge pour la nuit. Les nuages même s'écartent, les laissant

En hâte quittée cette terre qui tremble ils se sont regroupés dans la ville, bardés de portes.

Blue moraine in the glacier of evening

The grape goes back under the green, blue recaptures the sky, soil fades into the earth, red builds up and absorbs the fields of Crau. Colors free themselves from things and recover their thick and free reign before things, like the clay that predated Adam

The saurian earth emerges and lifts jaw to the moon, dreamy years come out of caves and prowl tenderly around the thick skin Cliff straightens up, Victoire recovers her age for the night. Even the clouds drift apart, leaving them

Hastily quitting this trembling earth they regroup in the town, bucklered by doors.

Le ciel comme un enfant monte en haut des arbres
L'eau devenue senteur
                              traverse
Les fleurs s'appellent Danaë dans le lit

Le bruit de Rome dans les cimes
                                                oscillantes
Ivres insectes   tonnelle des cris
Et le soleil mis en sacs légers ici
Et là
La peau s'irrite
Beauté d'arbre comme un cheval musclé sur la mare
Plus loin l'école de danse des jeunes pommiers

The sky like a child climbs high up the trees
The water become perfume
                              crosses
The flowers called Danaë in bed

The noise of Rome in the tops
                              swaying
Drunk insects   bower of cries
And the sun put in light bags here
And there
The skin itches
Beauty of a tree like a muscular horse over the pond
Further away the dancing school of young apple trees

Phases événements demi-voltes
Ellipses centaures prolepses cercles voltes
Élisions masques détails fuites instantanés
Comparaisons déplacements hyperboles explosions
Pointes quatre-coins passages câbrements
Colin-maillards figements torsions apostrophes
Équerres saute-moutons voilements ocelles
Véroniques thmèses écarquillements mimétisme
Pointes glissements synecdoques pas-de-deux
Grands-soleils jeters saluts quartes moues
Quart-de-tour supposition premiers-quartiers métonymie
Septimes paris grands-écarts bluffs ombres chinoises
Qui tendent à l'orateur sous son silence la figure

Vous appelez ça comparaison?

Phases events demivolts
Ellipses centaurs prolepses circles volts
Elisions masks details escapes snapshots
Comparisons displacements hyperboles explosions
Pointwork corner tag passages rearings
Blindman's bluff congealings torsions apostrophes
Squares leapfrog veilings ocelli
Veronicas tmeses eyes bulging mimicry
Pointwork slidings synecdoches pas-de-deux
Grand circles jetés greetings quartes pouts
Quarter turn supposition first quarters metonymy
Septimes bets splits bluffs shadow plays
That offer to the speaker under his silence the figure

You call that comparison?

lacis de centres dans le hall
Faisceaux des sorciers empaillés
Qui balaient cette arène ivres
Tournois de phares en jour nuptial
Chacune à traîne d'air, de paroles
A trousses de vie, des siens, d'ombres
Remonte vers le hall
Faisceaux de paille
Circulation diurne des cortèges
Réglés sur cette arène peu di
    tournoi des yeux qui poussent
L'air lent balayé par tes yeux frôle tournoie revire
Se croisent électrons gavotte vannerie
Se tressent dans le hall   Multi-
Mariages qui remontent chacun
Tout se prend à leurs traînes
Enfants la vie les siens ses ombres
Lacis de centres sur les dalles

entanglement of centers in the hall
Bundles of sorcerers stuffed with straw
Who sweep across this arena drunk
Beacon tournaments on a wedding day
Each with a train of air, of speech
With trunk hose of life, of her own people, of shadows
Going back up toward the hall
Bundles of straw
Diurnal processional traffic
Regulated to this arena hardly di
    tournament of eyes that push
The slow air swept by your eyes grazes spins veers again
Crossing each other electrons gavotte wickerwork
Braiding themselves in the hall   Multi-
Marriages that go back up each one
Everything catches in their trains
Children life their own their shadows
Entanglement of centers on the flagstones

Cette dame et sa belle fenêtre
Un ange asymétrique aux ailes porte-vent
disait je vous salue

L'amour distinguait l'absence et la mort

Dans la vie aux larges dimensions sans espoir de mourir
Vous êtes tellement une femme que vous vous posez comme une
femme

Que Béatrice soit aussi celle sur qui le temps touche un cheveu
Cette femme imaginaire qui a choisi mon signe

Mon augure l'a surprise dans les flammèches
Botticelli de sa chemise de jour enveloppée d'odeurs (pétrels et fous
de Bassan cultivent le mur qui borde la mer)
Elle est ce qui l'arrache à la mêlée
Il lui suffit d'en recevoir salut
Il ne hait plus il aime

Lente est la reconnaissance et que ces enfants nous succèdent et lente
la douceur d'une action bonne ou d'un coude de Loire et Loir

This lady and her beautiful window
An asymmetrical angel with wind-bearing wings
was saying I greet you

Love distinguished absence and death

In fully dimensional life with no hope of dying
You are so much a woman that you come forth as a woman

May Beatrice also be the one time touches a hair of
This imaginary woman who chose my sign

My augury took her by surprise in the Botticelli
Fire flakes of her day gown enveloped in odors (petrels and gannets
    from Bassan cultivate the wall that edges the sea)
She is what plucks him from the fray
It is enough for him to receive her greeting
He no longer hates he loves

Slow is recognition and that those children succeed us and slow the
    sweetness of a good act or of a bend in the Loire and the Loir

L'air la prend par la taille
La reste amoureux lui souffle les joues
Un tourneur peu visible achève ses bras
L'entour règle sa ronde sur ses hanches

Elle transpose la douceur dont les murs sont capables
Les choses s'arrangent comme ses femmes de chambre
Elle resserre la douceur dont sont capables les couleurs

Sa taille est l'horizon ses jambes les chemins ses bras le ciel
sa taille la lisière ses bras la perspective
Le vide lui fait des ailes
Les couleurs ses habits préparés sur les chaises son corset attentif

      Le monde est son danseur

The air takes her by the waist
The amorous remainder puffs out her cheeks
A barely visible turner finishes her arms
The surroundings time their round dances with her hips

She transposes the sweetness that the walls are capable of
Things arrange themselves as her chambermaids
She tightens the sweetness that colors are capable of

Her waist is the horizon her legs the paths her arms the sky
her waist the forest's edge her arms the perspective
The void makes wings for her
The colors her clothes laid out on the chairs her attentive corset

     The world is her dancing partner

Arrête ce moment où elle s'assied
Modérant la jupe à droite à gauche les yeux
Les jambes au fil sur le carrelage laissant
Les doigts se retrouver le corps pronominal

Sur l'axe où nous car nous sommes sur l'axe
Séjour d'habitude sous cieux oblong
Enceint de terre Il est besoin de baies dans le château
Y compris les lacets sur les murs
Et l'échappée grâce au leurre des jardins

Comme on regarde par le train
Où les fenêtres sont vastes et nombreuses
La marge de musique et pour les couleurs
Fut pratiqué le temple de toile

Hold this moment when she sits down
Moderating the skirt to the right to the left the eyes
The legs drifting on the tiles allowing
The fingers to find themselves again the pronomial body

On the axis where we—for we *are* on the axis
Customary sojourn under oblong skies
Surrounded by earth There is a need for bays in the chateau
Including the networks on the walls
And the vista thanks to the lure of the gardens

As one looks out the train
Where the windows are vast and numerous
The margin of music and for colors
The temple of canvas was contrived

A peine ouvre-t-elle trop ses lèvres par rire ou bâillement son visage
se perd dans la fosse des amygdales
Scrutant les muqueuses où s'abîme son nom l'amour glisse se raccro-
chant aux racines des seins Il se baisse et des eaux du cercle
d'anonymat saura faire remonter comme une nymphe la crase du
fils vers l'intelligence

No sooner does she open her lips too much from laughing or
    yawning than her face is lost in the trench of her tonsils
Scrutinizing the mucous membranes where her name is swallowed up
    love slides grabbing hold of the roots of her breasts He bends
    down and from waters of the circle of anonymity will know how
    to make the crasis of the son raise again like a nymph toward the
    intellect

Elle l'aide à passer sa chemise
Et l'extrémité de son âme les doigts
Prennent souci de ses bras de son corps
S'il n'y avait le détail du corps
L'âme votive à qui?

Jusqu'à ce qu'en tout point émergé
Prompt comme écaille il n'y ait plus
A réfléchir le ciel que mains attentives
Sans métonymie grâce au détail des muscles

She helps him on with his gown
And the extremity of his soul the fingers
Are careful of his arms of his body
If it were not for the detail of the body
To whom the votive soul?

Until at all emerged points
Prompt as scale there was nothing left
To reflect the sky but attentive hands
Without metonymy thanks to the muscles' details

Il est besoin d'un lecteur d'un geste d'un papier
D'un miroir Tu es visage ma feuille mon échancrure
Je suis le tissu pour que tu sois ton vide La surface
Pour que froisse la main L'aber où l'eau s'aiguise
Racine où le sol tressaille Ton blanc mon noir
Le creux pour ma difficulté le blanc pour que je sois
Ce dessin que je ne serais pas Tu es peau pour
Mon alphabet J'étais l'air pour que tu n'engorges
Alvéole pour que tu fusses arcade

There is a need for a reader for a gesture for a piece of paper
For a mirror You are face my leaf my indentation
I am the cloth so that you can be your void The surface
So that the hand rumples The fjord where the water hones itself
Root where the ground shudders Your white my black
The hollow for my difficulty the white so that I may be
This drawing that I would not be You are skin for
My alphabet I was the air so that you will not congest
Alveolus so that you may be arcade

Savoir pourquoi tu m'es si chère
ce bois charmant où les vaches sont passées
    Comme un enfant grâce à l'absence proportionnelle
    A la puissance de l'écart
ce bois mauve bordé de clairières où l'éclair a démis le chêne
    Quand tu t'éloignes comme une rive
    Tu gravites si près tout devient son
    Privé de rapport littéral
ce bois où l'embuscade du travail perce parfois l'épais
    Tandis que les enfants sont si distants
    Que leurs mots sont une fable
    Où ils parlent comme des humains
dure comme le moyeu des tourbes d'eau

    Heureux celui qui croit sans t'avoir vue
    Ta face cachée m'entoure alors
la pluie aux ongles de sœur aveugle sur la peau des châtaigniers

    J'écris pour que tu ne comprennes

To know why you are so dear to me
this charming woods where the cows have passed
    Like a child thanks to the proportional absence
    To the power of the space between
*this mauve woods bordered with clearings where lightning has
    dislocated the oak*
    When you withdraw like a bank
    You gravitate so close all becomes sound
    Deprived of literal connection
*this woods where the ambush of work occasionally pierces the
    thickness*
    While the children are so distant
    That their words are fable
    Where they speak like humans
hard as the hub of water peat

    Blesséd be the one who believes without having seen you
    Your hidden face surrounds me then
the rain with a blind sister's nails on the skin of the chestnut trees

    I write so that you do not understand

(*Les áges*)

Sa beauté la surface
L'idolâtrie de nos regards croisés
Mais de plus près la sueur de son nom perle
Pourtant «quelle heure est-il»
Alors j'adopte ses caries
Plus près   plus près
Le visage s'enfuit en rasant ses terres

Il y a l'image qu'ici je présente pour la première fois
En Grèce des crops étagés dans le torrent qui les lavait
Ceux dont les bords font leur délice
Mais ceux dont la courbe est la tunique de Nessos

Et ceci la question de la surface
Et du redoublement qui montre
La question du théâtre que le théâtre double
Et des coulisses les viscères et la station métaphysique
L'arroseur arrosé le médecin malade
Ce troisième homme qu'il multiplie
Pour comprendre les corps

Qu'est-ce qui se passe avec les femmes
Leur angle avec le sol leurs dents sur la voirie
Ce buste qu'elles allaitent en remontant la foule

     Enfant trouvé dans la mémoire
     Je la vois lentement grimée
     Le mal grandissait avec l'âge
     Plombs prunes étoiles passent
. . . .

D'âge où les pieds ne touchent pas le sol
Elle de bras en bras lévite
De mots en mots passe le poème
Et lui comme elle par protection

(*The ages*)

Her beauty the surface
The idolatry of our crossed gazes
But closer the sweat of her name beads
Nevertheless "what time is it"
Then I adopt her cavities
Closer   closer
My face takes off razing her lands

There is the image that I present here for the first time
In Greece bodies tiered in the torrent that washed them
Those for whom edges are delight
But those whose curve is the tunic of Nessus

And this the question of the surface
And of the redoubling which shows
The question of the theater that the theater doubles
And of the backstage the viscera and the metaphysical station
The waterer watered the sick doctor
This third man whom he multiplies
In order to understand bodies

What is it about women
Their angle with the ground their teeth on the thoroughfares
This bust they breastfeed pushing back through the crowd

    A foundling in one's memory
    I see her being made up slowly
    The disease was growing with age
    Pellets plums stars pass
. . . .

At the age when the feet do not touch the ground
She levitates from arm to arm
From word to word the poem passes
And it like her through the influence

Des paumes du foyer où ils sont innocents,
De l'espace qui les porte ignares d'angle en angle

Le sens fait signe par ses mains
Elle apprivoise S et I se posent
Sur les poings la nuque les épaules
O bague sa bouche G la prend à la gorge
. . . .

    Amante comme un os
    J'ai pitié de nous
    Les sourcils se compliquent
    La pensée passe comme un dauphin
    —le cillement le pouls la marche
    Je ne peux m'éloigner
    —faible fort et pause et faible fort et pause
    «Les feuilles sur la place les enfants de l'école»
    Apposition que surveille le *comme*
    Tandis qu'attend son tour inévitable
    L'analogie qui nous expulse de ce monde

Bruit de guerre lasse au ciel
Proche mais déviée comme les routes nouvelles
Les âges s'apaisent au jardin
Stagnants mêlés aux statues
L'eau ne manque ni ne déborde
Des oiseaux verts s'en détournent
Aux genoux des femmes du gravier le soleil supplie

Ne laisse pour le compte
Le jardinier roulé sur son échelle roulante
Assis parmi les cimes avec sa faux
Ni les linges de la cure sous le porche bleu

    Le poème *commue*
    La peine en roseau
    La pudeur en laurier
    Le meurtre en perdrix
    C'est un nom composé

Of the open palms of the home where they are innocent,
Of the space that carries them ignorant from angle to angle

Meaning signals through her hands
She tames S and I place themselves
On her fists her nape her shoulders
O ring her mouth G grabs her by the throat
. . . .

    Lover like a bone
    I pity us
    The eyebrows become complicated
    Thought passes like a dolphin
    —the blink the pulse the walking
    I cannot go away
    —unstressed stressed and pause unstressed stressed and pause
    "The leaves on the square the school children"
    Apposition that the *like* surveys
    While the analogy that expels us from this world
    Awaits its inevitable turn

Worn-out war noise in the sky
Near but deviated like the new highways
The ages grow calm in the garden
Stagnant mixed with statues
There's neither lack of water nor overflowing
Green birds turn away from it
At the knees of the gravel's women the sun begs

Don't leave for the account
The gardener rolled along on his rolling ladder
Seated among the tree tops with his scythe
Nor the vicarage linen under the blue porch

    The poem *commutes*
    The sentence into reed
    Modesty into laurel
    Murder into partridge
    It is a noun composed

Avec le côté *pierre* des pierres
Les prénoms des vivants
La moue en *ure* de luxure
Avoine et pivoine siamoisés sur le champ
—et de toute façon la distance
Qui sépare les linges
Du poème privé de genèse

L'aïeule déjà bordée de glaïeuls
Avec les yeux de mon père étonnés
Que la porte délivre ce visage qu'eut un fils
Elle meurt en songeant au voyage de Nice

With the *stone* aspect of stones
The first names of the living
The pout in the *ewd* of lewdness
Sweet pea and peony siamesed on the field
—and in any case the distance
Separating the linen
From the poem bereft of genesis

The old lady already bordered by gladioli
With my father's eyes astonished
That the door delivers this face that a son had
Dies dreaming of the trip to Nice

de *Actes*
from *Acts*

L'échappée

comme on ouvre une fenêtre   soudain   comme on éclaire un sentier   elle se mettait au piano ainsi   comme on esquisse un pas de danse une marelle dans la rue   comme on bat des paupières une fois de trop ou des doigts sur le velours comme on tourne les pouces, comme on fait tout: «pour rien»; comme on regarde par le train où les fenêtres sont vastes et nombreuses, la musique en marge, et pour les couleurs fut institué le carré de toile c'est toujours pour voir plus loin là-bas

(une vue pour chaque sens et tous les changements d'échelle de la poésie pour exercer la mème vision)

elle ouvrait soudain cette fenêtre sur l'axe spatial où nous car nous sommes sur l'axe ce séjour d'habitude que nous appelons réel le sousmarin oblong enceint de terre et il est besoin d'ouvrir toutes les fenêtres au matin dans le château

(et chaque vue est métaphorique en ce sens que voyant le tout par son angle et cherchant à dire les autres aux autres et leurs rapports par son biais)

ainsi comme on pousse un camarade comme on pose la plume comme on (n') écoute (pas) celui qui parle (quelle est cette indifférence à la négation, qui ne change rien à ce qui doit être dit), comme on se renverse en arrière, comme on pêche à la ligne, comme on feuillette le livre ou le jour à travers la jalousie vénitienne

(nous aide donc à *voir* tout moyen qui réplique la forme feuilletée du volet)

comme on écoute l'oiseau

ainsi elle se mettait à son piano et déroulait la phrase   l'avenue brève d'un Mozart où nous la suivions (le trompe-l'œil ne «trompe» que l'œil premier, l'œil affairé qui cherche le plus court chemin, mais il induit, grâce à ce leurre qu'il est, l'autre œil vers l'échelle latérale, le théâtre à côté)

y compris les lacets fébriles sur le papier, et les graffiti à tous les murs, pour amener à tout panneau en toute demeure comme on accroche une carte postale, la vue symbolique du reste

une certaine échappée.

Vista

as one opens a window   suddenly   as one lights up a path she
sat down at the piano thus   as one runs through a dance step   a
hopscotch in the street   as one bats one's eyelids once too often or
one's fingers on velvet as one twiddles one's thumbs, as one does
everything: "for nothing"; as one looks out the train where the
windows are vast and numerous, the music in the margin, and for
colors the square of canvas was instituted it is always to see further
out down there
        (a view for each sense and all of poetry's changes of scale in order
to exercise the same vision)
        she opened suddenly that window on the spatial axis where we
for we are on the axis   this stay that usually we call real the oblong
submarine surrounded by earth and it is necessary in the morning
to open all the windows in the chateau
        (and every view is metaphoric in the sense that seeing everything
from its own angle and trying to say the others to the others and
their connections through its slant
        thus as one gives a schoolmate a shove as one puts down one's
pen as one does (not) listen to the one who's talking (what is that
indifference to negation, which changes nothing about what is to
be said), as one leans back, as one goes angling, as one leafs through
a book or a day aslant the venetian blind
        (helps us thus to *see* every means that retorts the leaflike form of
the shutter)
        as one listens to the bird
        thus she sat down at the piano and unrolled the phrase   the brief
avenue of a Mozart where we were following her (the trompe-l'œil
only "trumps" the primary eye, the busy eye looking for the shortest
path, but it leads, thanks to the lure that it is, the other eye toward
the lateral scale, the theatre near by)

        including the feverish windings on the paper, and the graffiti on
all the walls, in order to bring to every panel, in every residence as
one tacks up a postcard, the symbolic view of the rest
                                            a certain vista.

J'appelle *muse* la bascule du ciel, le vent transbordeur à *son* gré de nos vues, ce lavis quand j'entrouvre avec le chat mes yeux, celle qui l'a caressé ; *muse*, la profusion que les œuvres rangent en séquence inachevable de concertos, en poèmes réitérés, en file indienne, à plat, et classée entassée sur toiles, sur pierres, sur bois, sur papier à musique, in-octavo de Linné, vitrines d'Aristote, dossiers

J'appelle *muse* la douleur qu'ils me causent, la jonglerie de lune et de soleil, *muse* le voyage au sud de la terre où les lacs glacés sont bordés de flamands roses comme les ongles faits sur l'éventail du crépuscule, la lune et son cortège de mares quand elle traverse nuptiale le pont de la terre pareille au Chili d'un extrême à l'autre, *muse* les grues le taureau noir une chouette passa les cygnes, la villel plus australe où je fus s'appelant *Porvenir*, l'oiseau pubis, le cheval de mer pourrissait sous la croix dextrogyre des mouettes, *muse* le voyage, la Terre de Feu comme un nuage au bout de la rue de *Punta-Arenas*, la main royale de la mer, l'avion comme un œil élégant, la patience de Noé qu'il fallut pour saluer la révérence aussi longue que le jour de la mer magellane, le nuage où le ciel voilait son amour et le portique de couleurs où il passa, au retour le rivage patagon comme un coq

muse le voyage moral où les rêves sont de jour et le courage croissant dans le dos, l'exactitude poétique de la terre qui passe par la tête, la nuit de Pampa révélant la distance, la table sans femme où chacun doute de parler, ce palier de calme à une certaine profondeur du tourment, la patience des couleurs qui assiste à nos choix, la nappe d'humus remise tous les matins, le val qu'il faut descendre

                               faux de cendres
l'homonymie flegmatique en la langue qui est joconde comme l'effigie fameuse, l'hospitalière paronomase semblable au puzzle abandonné par les enfants, l'acceptation où toute chose repose dans l'ambiguïté du génitif, l'érosion toujours originale qui tire du latin l'espagnol et le portugais

muse le cerveau tendre où tout échappe, la disette octroyée au diseur, l'audace à laquelle s'offre la grammaire, *muse* ma confiance au non-vouloir penser, les réponses migratrices, l'égalité qui tombe

I call *muse* the seesaw of the sky, the wind transshipper at *his* volition of our views, this tinting when I open with the cat my eyes a slit, the one who caressed the cat; *muse*, the profusion that works range in uncompletable concerto sequences, in reiterated poems, in Indian file, flattened, and classified piled up on canvases, on stones, on wood, on music paper, in Linnaeus's octavos, Aristotle's glass cases, files

I call *muse* the pain that they cause me, the moon sun jugglery, *muse* the voyage to the south of the earth where frozen lakes are bordered by flamingos pink as the painted nails of the fan of twilight, the moon and its cortege of ponds when nuptially it crosses the bridge of the earth similar to Chile from one extreme to the other, *muse* the cranes the black bull an owl passed the swans, the most southern town where I was which called itself *Porvenir*, the pubis bird, the sea horse was rotting under the dextrogyre cross of gulls, *muse* the voyage, Tierra del Fuego like a cloud at the end of *Punta-Arenas* Street, the royal hand of the sea, the airplane like an elegant eye, the patience of Noah necessary to greet the daylong curtsy of the Magellan Sea, the cloud with which the sky veiled its love and the portico of colors through which it passed, on return the Patagonian shore like a cock

muse the moral voyage where dreams are daydreams and courage growing in one's back, the poetic exactitude of the earth crossing one's mind, the Pampa night disclosing the distance, womanless table at which each doubts if he will speak, this platform of calm at a certain depth in the torment, the patience of colors that help us make our choice, the humus tablecloth put away each morning, the vale one must descend

      mist to sand

                 the phlegmatic homonymy in the language that is gioconda like the famous effigy, the hospitable paronomasia similar to the jigsaw puzzle abandoned by the children, the acceptance where everything reposes in genitive ambiguity, the always original erosion which draws Spanish and Portuguese out of Latin

comme la neige sur les «moindres événements» que tout soit vrai y
compris «la trompeuse tendresse de l'adieu»

muse que la montée soit montée dans le corps et la descente
descente dans le corps, *muse* derechef l'âme étrange et les conditions,
les poèmes que nous lisons chez le dentiste, en battant du pied pour
couvrir le sang, à l'étalage du hasard les poèmes qui résistent au
feuillettement du pouls; *muse* le repas qui est toujours *servi là* en
ce conte *La Belle et la Bête* où nous vivons, car «il descendit dans
le jardin et trouva préparé le repas»

J'appelle *muse* Venise les porches nègres à rubans Venise aux
ongles gondolés où l'étranger se retourne comme celui qui arrive à
Venise amenée au visible par miracle la place comme un carré de
joueurs les choses qui se regardent car le visible est une affaire
d'hommes

muse l'égal emplissement de tous les lieux, cette frise riche du
détroit égale à nos yeux étroits la liberté spacieuse de l'espace libre,
que tout parvis toute esplanade toute terrasse tout perron «dégage»
pour montrer, cette multiplicité discrète qui nous laisse entrer et
sortir, quitter, nous rapprocher, «je ne vous dérange pas», *muse* ce
vide

muse l'histoire des muses, les témoignages chroniques, toute nais-
sance fée un chevet situé sous neuf dons de marraines provinciales
irréfutables, l'histoire maintenant ce collage de *nouvelles* et le plan
incliné des inventions, la venue tout à fait surprenante de Philoctete
ou de Joyce, la geste imprévisible d'Achille ou du Tintoret

Tinte teinte Orée Auray tente forêt stentor Aretin Perroquet Tyn-
dare Paindoré Tintoret

l'excessive promesse des noms, l'innommé des espèces encore
cachées qui attendent leur tour de monter à la clairière des hommes

J'appelle cette noce tardive qu'il faut veiller, cette absence festivale
dont le feu là-bas soutient nos lampes vierges, *muse* donc son avent,
sa préfiguration à saccades gris doré de pintades

les greffes délicates de mémoire dans la nuit, la légende d'un mot,
muse aussi l'ennemi, la haine qui froisse l'entrevue, cette poignée
d'os faux et de grimaces, ce consistant alliage de derme et d'humeur
qui poursuit loin de moi la relation des densités, l'indifférence à ma
mort, le retard des hommes à transformer en loi leur élément, la

muse the tender brain where everything escapes, the shortage granted to the storyteller, the audacity to which grammar lends itself, *muse* my confidence in not willing thinking, the migratory responses, the equality which falls like snow on the "slightest events," that everything is true including "the deceitful tenderness in the farewell"

muse that the climbing be climbing in the body and the descent descent in the body, *muse* once again the strange soul and the conditions, the poems that we read at the dentist's, tapping a foot to cover the blood, at the display of chance the poems that resist the leafing pulse; *muse* the meal that is always *served there* in this tale of *Beauty and the Beast* where we live, for "he went down into the garden and found the meal prepared"

I call *muse* Venice the porches Negroes in ribbons Venice of the gondolaed nails where the stranger turns around like the one arriving in Venice led to the visible by a miracle the plaza like a square of players the things that look at each other for the visible is a human concern

muse the equal filling up of all places, that rich frieze of the strait equal to our straightened eyes, the spacious liberty of free space, that every parvis every esplanade every terrace every stoop "clears" so as to show, this discrete multiplicity that allows us to enter and to leave, to go away, to approach, "I'm not disturbing you," *muse* this void

muse the history of the muses, the chronic testimonies, every birth a fairy a bedside located under nine gifts of irrefutable provincial godmothers, history now this collage of *news* and the inclined plane of inventions, the utterly surprising coming of Philoctetes or of Joyce, the unforeseeable gesture of Achilles or of Tintoretto

Ting tint Orée Auray tent forest stentor Aretino Parrot Tyndareus Paindoré Tintoretto

the excessive promise of names, the namelessness of still hidden species which wait their turn to rise to the clearing of men

I summon this tardy wedding that must be waked, this festival absence whose fire down there supports our virgin lamps, *muse* therefore her advent, her prefiguration with guinea fowl gilded grey jerks

froideur du bonheur pour le savoir, toute la configuration des hiatus, des étais, des percées dans l'édifice involontaire du séjour, l'épaule pétrifiée de la main qui inscrit *mane thecel pharès*

the delicate grafts of memory in the night, the legend of a word, *muse* likewise the enemy, the hate that crumples the interview, this handful of fake bones and grimaces, this solid alloy of derma and humour that pursues far from me the relationship between densities, the indifference to my death, the slowness of men in transforming their element into a law, the frigidity of happiness for knowledge, all the configurations of hiatuses, of props, of breaks in the involuntary edifice of the stay, the petrified shoulder of the hand that writes *mene tekel upharsin*

Au soir sur l'autre berge cigales constellées

Aérolithes ici dans l'atmosphère des lampes

Entre tourne Océan le grand fleuve encaissé

At night on the far shore the constellated cicadas

Aerolites here in the atmosphere of the lamps

Ocean the great embanked river turns between

de *Figurations*
from *Figurations*

Belles emphases

L'eau n'aime que le ciel
Ne veut voir Se renverse
A toute pause Que lui
Ne cherche d'autre preuve

Combien de morts combien de vivants
Dans leur trou dans leur geôle
Ont désiré désirent ce qui est là
Le resserrement spacieux des Trois
Où l'arbre est le précurseur sombre

Comme les bords d'une onde d'onde ainsi
Nous les proches d'une fille une amante et de même
Qu'il y a science de cette onde labile de même
Analyse de l'âme notre vide Qu'arrive-t-il
Au cri poussé depuis mille secondes mille ans

Raisonnons   Il doit bien
Y avoir un poème
Tel que pour cette heure et cette sorte de contagion
D'on ne sait quoi de comparable de porche en porche

Cette rumeur de soir de rive de retour
Il touche un plus grand nombre d'hommes
Alors   Commence   Avance un mot puis l'autre
Encore   Marche   Lâche les mains   Mettons
Le Pacifique dans le coup—dernière antiphrase
La plus vaste trois cinquièmes de la terre à réduire

Qu'il puisse s'asseoir cela est paix
Parmi les autres comme Pasternak
Avec les chiens de face aux pieds de pluie
Hôte écrivant les bruits avec les chiens
Admis sur le carrelage
Tant que ne cesse pas le désir de survivre

Beautiful Emphases

The water loves only the sky
It wants to see (It overturns
At every pause) Only the sky
It looks for no other proof

How many dead how many living
In their "hole" in their jail
Have desired desire that which is there
The spacious contracting of the Three
Where the tree is the dark precursor

Like the edges of a wave of a wave thus
We the relatives of a daughter a lover and in the same
Way there is a science of this labile wave in the same
Analysis of the soul our emptiness What happens
To the cry uttered a thousand seconds ago a thousand years

Think it through   There really must
                Be a poem there
Such as for this hour and this sort of contagion
Of what one doesn't know in what way comparable from porch to
    porch

This hum of evening of bank of return
It touches a greater number of men
In that case   Begin   Advance one word then another
Still   Walk   Release your hands   Get
The Pacific in on it—the last antiphrasis
The most vast 3/5ths of the earth to reduce

That he can sit down that is peace
Among the others like Pasternak
With the dogs facing with feet of rain
Host writing the sounds with the dogs
        Admitted on the tiled floor
        While the desire to survive does not cease

BEAUTIFUL EMPHASES   111

Etc.

La lune dix-cors, amazone, ou ce vieux maître d'hôtel ubiquiste qui fait le tour de notre mois, penché sur nos tables comme une légende, chauve ici, mais rengorgé, la serviette sur l'épaule

là-bas lune œstrocultrice, plus visible d'ici que le Penjab, et va d'un cloître à l'autre, les grilles découpent nos faces, elle est sans méridien, nous la chargeons de nos télécommunications, notre invariant

tessère sublime qui se fragmente régulièrement, ses phases gagent l'hospitalité, du nord au sud nous échangeons quartiers de lune, nos fils se reconnaissent

une dernière fois la lune vulgaire une dernière fois pour nous dire cela, d'amazone ou de maître d'hôtel ou son apparition entre les arbres pour Eustache, etc., une dernière fois ce jeu—ou bien faut-il *rayer les mentions inutiles* et ne laisser que

« Le volume de la lune est cinquante fois petit que celui de la terre, dont elle se trouve à une distance moyenne de 384 400 km »

ni voyante ni Hausfreund ni visiteuse ni cervidée ni Nuktiphaès peri gaian alômenon allotrion phôs

n'est-elle la muette sur le toit de Brecht, la lucide extra dont la ruse nous dévêt?

à son clou tacite ne déposons-nous nos mots sans un mot d'elle contre tous les autres   son silence nous fait avouer, nous lui offrons baignoires, psychés, bijoux, hécatombe de lexiques   elle favorise le commerce poétique

Etc.

The 10-pointer moon, an amazon, or this old ubiquitous head waiter who wanders around our month, bending over our tables like a legend, bald here, but full of himself, napkin over shoulder

over there an oestricultivatress, more visible from here than the Punjab, she goes from one cloister to another, the gates cut our faces, she is without meridian, we put her in charge of our telecommunications, our invariant

sublime tessera which regularly fragments, her phases guarantee hospitality, from North to South we exchange quarters of the moon, our sons recognize each other

for the last time the common moon for the last time to tell us that, of an amazon or of a head waiter, or her apparition among the trees for Eustace etc., for the last time this game—or must we *delete when appropriate* and leave only

"The volume of the moon is fifty times smaller than that of the earth, from which it is at an average distance of 175,000 miles"

neither a clairvoyant nor a Hausfreund nor a visitor nor a cervida nor Nuktiphaès peri gaian alômenon allotrion phôs

isn't she the mute on Brecht's roof, the lucid extra whose ruse undresses us?

on her tacit nail don't we deposit our words without a word from her in exchange against all the others   her silence makes us confess, we offer her bathtubs, swing mirrors, jewels, a hecatomb of lexicons   she patronizes the poetry business

encaisse
d'argent au chapiteau de chaque municipe, contrepartie de nos
traductions déposée ostensible innégociable comma un zénith elle
gage nos traités et soutient toute dette

        une dernière fois je vous
avertis, que se passe-t-il depuis que nous l'approchons . . . Cette
chose absente qui n'est rien se prête à tout, plaque blanche tournante
des noms et des sens, cette chose emphytéotique incessible tout à
fait présente, innommable, elle passe sous silence mais insignifiante
et ainsi là c'est elle

       lune là et à cette distance—accessible
aujourd'hui mais inapprochable toujours au terrestre—en excès sur
toute nomination son sort touche nos fronts et ce que nous les
diserts disons de plus dément ne lui convient pas mal

         ongle barque
chasteté lunule licorne serpe chasseresse étable dune anagramme de
nulle

   ses récidives distendent les glossaires elle relance la roue des
oraisons des beaux entretiens nous y passerons tous aucun arrange-
ment n'est à rayer il n'est de mot qui ne défile adéquat ne soit
monnaie jetée sur sa pierre de touche
  «Il y a plus de choses dans le ciel, etc.» Cela veut dire? Que les
choses n'étant pas toutes sur le même plan, les moins à portée des
mains sont modèles qu'aucune n'est simplement à portée de main:

       mais elles s'étagent se raréfient
montent jusqu'aux étoiles s'espaçant de moins en moins sûres
jusqu'à la couronne de nombres (et d'autre part se cachant en
l'opaque se tassant entre les antipodes se réservent serrées) de plus
en plus indifférentes en leur exposition astronomique détachées «in-
évitables» idoles induisant la litanie des langues:

  Des astres des forêts et d'Achéron l'honneur
  Diane au monde hault moyen et bas préside

silver reserve at
the capital of every township, counterpart of our translations de-
posited ostensible nonnegotiable like a zenith she guarantees our
treaties and backs up every debt

for the last time I warn you, what
is happening since we have approached her . . . This absent thing
which is nothing lends herself to everything, white turntable of
names and of meanings, this emphyteutic thing untransferable com-
pletely present, unnameable, she passes over in silence but insignifi-
cant and so there   it's her

moon there and at that distance—acces-
sible today but unapproachable always for terrestrials—exceeding
all naming   her fate touches our foreheads and the most demented
things that we talkative ones say don't suit her badly

fingernail barque
chastity lunule unicorn billhook huntress stable dune anagram of
anul

her reappearances distend glossaries she respins the wheel of
prayers of wonderful talks we all have to go through it no combina-
tion is to be struck out there is no word that does not file past
appropriate no word not a coin tossed onto her touchstone
"There are more things in heaven etc." That means something?
That since things are not all on the same level, those least within
hand's reach are models that none of them are simply within hand's
reach:

but they tierify rarify rise up to the stars distancing less and
less sure up to the crown of numbers (and on the other hand hiding
in opacity settling between the antipodes keeping compact) more
and more indifferent in their astronomic exposition detached "inevit-
able" idols inducting the litany of languages:

By the stars by the forests and by Acheron honored
Diana in the high the mid and the low world presides

ETC.   115

Et ses chevaux ses chiens ses Euménides guide
Pour esclairer chasser donner mort et horreur
. . . .

Ses flambans forts et griefs feux filez et encombres
Lune Diane Hécate aux cieux terre et enfers
Ornant questant genant nos Dieux nous et nos ombres

une dernière fois sommes requis de nous arrêter au rapport du
scarabée et du soleil

(l'inconsciente feinte de la philosophie affectant
de croire que la perception voyait la lune se coucher «à deux cents
pas» (?) notons-y plutôt le symptôme aberrant à ses lèvres d'un
secret refoulé qui parle travesti, en haillons parmi nous vestige aplati
de la figure ancienne, en attente que lui lave les traits son éclat
jodellien,

car dans la version antique la lune le soleil, nulle «erreur
des sens» ne les vit se coucher à la belle étoile au bout du village
dans l'emplacement réservé aux nomades)

une dernière fois plutôt
sommes sommés de nous arrêter au soleil comme scarabée, au scara-
bée comme soleil, puisqu'il ne s'est jamais agi d'une mauvaise ap-
préciation, d'une confusion d'ignare optique pour prendre en pa-
tience l'avent de la science correctrice

mais triangle mystique comme
d'omphale et de crêtes iliaques, le soleil l'œil le scarabée sommets
équidistants incommensurables: la différence contractée d'origine
en figure entre l'œil et le scarabée, entre le soleil et l'œil, entre le
soleil et le scarabée, le silence de cet infini a de quoi emphaser

O ressemblance pays d'adoption
Tes faces ne ressemblent et qui ainsi ressemblent
Le volume de mer s'explicite
Un merle enchante son territoire
Le corps se dira par le corps:

116   ETC.

And her horses her dogs her Eumenides she guides
So as to light up to hunt to create death and horror
. . . .

Her strong flames and grievances fires nets and fetters
Moon Diana Hecate in heaven earth and hell
Adorning questing hindering our Gods us and our shadows

for the last time we are required to focus on the rapport between the scarab and the sun

(the unconscious sham of philosophy pretending to believe that perception saw the moon setting "two hundred steps away" (?) let us note rather the aberrant symptom on her lips of a repressed secret which speaks transvestite, in rags among us flattened vestige of the ancient figure, waiting for her Jodelian blaze to wash her features,

for in the antique version the moon the sun, no "error of the senses" observed them sleeping under the stars at the town's end in the area reserved for nomads)

for the last time rather we are summoned to concentrate on the sun as a scarab, on the scarab as a sun, since it has never been a case of bad judgment, of a confused optical ignorance to patiently await the advent of correcting science

but a mystical triangle like that of the omphalus and the iliac crests, the sun the eye the scarab equidistant incommensurable summits: the difference contracted from the beginning into a figure between the eye and the scarab, between the sun and the eye, between the sun and the scarab, the silence of this infinity has something to emphasize

O resemblance adopted country
Your faces don't resemble and which thus resemble
The volume of the sea is explicit about itself
A blackbird enchants his territory

ETC.   117

Les cheveux (comme un coup de sang
d'arquebuse des os)   .   .   .

   silence

       banc de silence les oreilles s'arrêtent l'ouïe a des fourmis
non l'œil ne se prend pas pour le sujet le plus intéressant son tuteur
l'émancipe à ce moment: la lune dix-cors redoublée en son propre
halo comme un cadre d'icône surgit entre les arbres de la chasse

silence

mes amis («mes amis»)

        à quoi bon céder au mutisme de lune, perte en
l'œil et qui ressort plus bas entre la bouche bavarde citant toutes
les langues du monde à son anonymat comme le cerf iconophore
bifurqué buisson mobile entre les branches, son silence autorise tous
les mots les paniers de roseaux les métaux les flûtes les peintres des
signes intaris comme les bains où elle ne se trempe pas, la sphinge
sans question le sein rond confondu à la face et ainsi sans réponse
et sans mot est-ce un grain de café un Φ un sexe un Θ elle rôde
comme ce qu'on ne parvient à se rappeler, le plus proche, le pense-
homme souviens-toi qu'il y a quelque chose

        et quand nous arriverons
sur son «sol» ensoleillé, alors *alunir atterrir*—déjà l'hésitation pour
la métaphore tressaille—nous apportons nos mots, y trouverons nos
ponces notre relief récidivant nos fictions comme partout réinjectant
un petit homme dans le grand, emboîtant nos esprits animaux dans
ses cavités («*la cause formelle de l'ivresse consiste en la quantité
surabondante et la qualité de vapeurs chaudes et humides, qui s'élè-
vent de la substance du vin, lesquelles venant à remplir le cerveau
et ses ventricules et de là s'épandant à l'origine des nerfs et touchant
leurs conduits, excitent en l'homme le sommeil de l'ivresse tenant
par leur humidité les esprits animaux liés, attachés et assoupis*»)

nous

entrerons dans le cerveau à peu près à la même époque atterrissant
ainsi en nos deux satellites crâne et lune

118   ETC.

The body will be spoken through the body:
Hair (like an uprush of blood
from a bone crossbow)
                              .   .   .

   silence
            school of silence the ears stop the hearing tingles asleep no
the eye does not take itself to be the most interesting subject its
tutor emancipates it at this moment: the 10-pointer moon redoubled
within its own halo like an icon frame surges between the trees of
the hunt

                                                              silence
my friends ("my friends")

                    why give in to the mutism of the moon,
loss in the eye which reappears lower between the talkative lips
summoning all the languages in the world before her anonymity
like the icon-bearing bifurcated stag mobile bush between the
branches, the moon's silence authorizes all words reed baskets metals
flutes painters of inexhaustible signs like baths in which she doesn't
even get her feet wet, Madame Sphinx without a question the round
breast confused with her face and thus without response and word-
less is it a coffee bean a Φ a sexual organ a Θ the moon prowls like
something that one cannot remember, what is closest, the mammary
jogger remember that there is something

                         and when we arrive on
her sunlit "ground," then *to moon to land*—already the hesitation
regarding the metaphor trembles—we bring our words, we'll find
there our pumices our relief recurring our fictions as everywhere
reinjecting a big man with a little one, fitting our animal spirits into
her cavities ("*the formal cause of drunkenness consists in the
superabundant quantity and in the quality of warm and humid
vapors, which rise from the substance of the wine, which upon filling
the brain and its ventricles and spreading thence to the origin of the
nerves and touching their passages, excite in man the sleep of drunken-
ness keeping the animal spirits bound, attached and deadened through
their humidity*")

                                        ETC.   119

mais encore établis dans leur intervalle ne pouvant nous retourner nous-mêmes vivant le gant de peau d'âme

métaphorisant tout à notre approche occidentaux peut-être (naguère en Amazonie le même transport, nomination les mêmes questions sur la race et l'incarnation et le souffle immortel conquête échangeant le sel et le sang)

parler mes amis comme si on ne devait plus se revoir, d'une manière telle que se revoir soit inutile, posthumément d'ici, de choses telles parce qu'on ne se reverra plus

we'll get into the brain in about the same epoch
landing thus on our two satellites skull and moon

but still set in their interval unable to turn over by ourselves
alive the glove of soul skin

metaphoring everything at our approach
occidentals perhaps (formerly in Amazonia the same transport nomi-
nation the same questions about race and incarnation and the immor-
tal breath a conquest trading salt and blood)

to speak my friends as
if we were never to meet again, in such a way that seeing each other
again would be useless, posthumously from here, of such things
because we never will see each other again

L'été l'hiver la nuit la nuit

La terre tombe en parachute
Les deltas du sang se jettent à l'air
Auréoles éperonnent les têtes
Et les empreintes digitales de la mer sont respectées

L'hiver n'intéressait personne
Les livres gonflés de défiance
Recueillent seuls *les anges de nos campagnes*
Nous lapidant le soleil affaibli
Refîmes apaisés les gestes du déluge
(charge d'enfant sur l'humérus)

Né à né dans le lit
La main reconnaît la carte d'un corps
Se chiffrent en nous les ondes d'une eau vicinale
Cette boue héritée
Ce fut un seul jour par monts et vals

Lumière sous l'horizon du monde voisin qui passe
Remonte vers l'actrice de nuit cernée Véga
Comme Yvette Guilbert ou les cils d'un Degas

Summer Winter the Night the Night

The earth falls by parachute
The deltas of blood spurt into the air
Halos spur the heads
And the fingerprints of the sea are respected

Winter did not interest anyone
The books inflated with defiance
Alone receive *the angels of our fields*
We stoning the weakened sun
Reenacted appeased the gestures of the flood
(a child burden on the humerus)

Born to born in the bed
The hand recognizes the map of a body
Coded in us the waves of a by-water
This inherited mud
This was a single day over hill and dale

Light under the horizon of the neighboring world which passes
Reascends toward the night actress eye-ringed Vega
Like Yvette Guilbert or the eyelashes of a Degas

Prose

Tu me manques mais maintenant
Pas plus que ceux que je ne connais pas
Je les invente criblant de tes faces
La terre qui fut riche en mondes
(Quand chaque roi guidait une île
A l'estime de ses biens (cendre d'
Oiseaux, manganèse et salamandre)
Et que des naufragés fédéraient les bords)

Maintenant tu me manques mais
Comme ceux que je ne connais pas
Dont j'imagine avec ton visage l'impatience
J'ai jeté tes dents aux rêveries
Je t'ai traité par-dessus l'épaule

(Il y a des vestales qui reconduisent au Pacifique
Son eau fume C'est après le départ des fidèles
L'océan bave comme un mongol aux oreillers du lit
Charogne en boule et poils au caniveau de sel
Un éléphant blasphème Poséidon)

Tu ne me manques pas plus que ceux
Que je ne connais pas maintenant
Orphique tu l'es devenu J'ai jeté
Ton absence démembrée en plusieurs vals
Tu m'as changé en hôte Je sais
Ou j'invente

Prose

I miss you but now
No more than those whom I do not know
I invent them riddling with your faces
The earth once rich in worlds
(When each king guided an island
By dead-reckoning its wealth (bird
Ash, manganese and salamander)
And castaways federated the shores)

Now I miss you but
Like those whom I do not know
Whose impatience I imagine with your face
I have flung your teeth to reveries
I have dealt with you over my shoulder

(There are vestals who escort back to the Pacific
Its water steams The faithful have already departed
The ocean drools like a mongol to his bed pillows
Balled up carrion and skins in the salt trough
An elephant blasphemes Poseidon)

I don't miss you more than those
Whom I do not know now
Orphic you've become I have flung
Your dismembered absence into several vales
You've turned me into a guest I know
Or I invent

Quadratures

Oiseau de proie aux boucles anniversaires ce matin les dés furent jetés dans l'ellipse à foyer terre à foyer inconnu, tout refait un tour: vase qui recueille l'urine, lucarne ovale du ciel, parapluie sauvette où les cravates se déplient, l'éventail mâle, les cartes obscènes accouchées de la manche, le plan sur la table où se penchent les maîtres, l'antidosis sur la fosse boursière, tores échangés aux annulaires, vestiges roses des chapeaux, et l'orbe au geste d'intendant; l'aubier ceinture le tonneau où résonne le conseil courbe des Cortès, les paumes rejouent le manteau rouge tandis que vire le cosmonaute rivé à l'orbite, Atlas roulé sur les lignes de niveau de la Perse

les deux races divergent

du chasseur de sarcelles qui se console de transmettre la mort à des fils et d'en être puni, puisqu'à cent pas de la maison les cris se changent en roseaux, la nuit refond le nid

et de l'autre qui souffre et rien n'arriverait sans sa démence, sa cave où croît tout levain d'injustice, sa face d'apiculteur où se rassemble l'essaim

les deux races convergent

6 h.   L'aimé du soleil, l'autre côté des nuages
Le pavement d'aucun oiseau: quand il s'entrouvre
Terre est au fond d'une perte qui regorge
Le soleil y descend vertes échelles
Lichen dérivent entre deux airs les brumes
Un banc de pies sur fond de tiges
Où les maisons polies reposent

8 h.
Quand l'arbre éventé revire
Comme les branches du tigre
En tous sens rivé

Quadratures

Bird of prey with anniversarial loops this morning the dice were thrown into the ellipse its foyer earth its foyer unknown, everything makes another turn: vessel that collects urine, oval lucarne of the sky, double-quick umbrella where the neckties unfold, the male fan, the obscene postcards born to the sleeve, the map on the table over which the masters stoop, the antidosis over the grant holder pit, toris exchanged on ring fingers, pink vestiges from hats, and the orb with an intendant's gesture; the sapwood girdles the barrel where the curved Cortes council resounds, the palms replay the red mantle while the cosmonaut veers riveted to the orbit, Atlas rolled over the land contours of Persia

the two races diverge

of the teal

hunter who consoles himself for transmitting death to sons and for being punished for it, since a hundred steps from the house the cries change into reeds, night recasts the nest

and of the other who suf-

fers and nothing would happen without his madness, his cellar where the whole leaven of injustice rises, his beekeeper face where the swarm gathers

the two races converge

6 a.m.   Beloved by the sun, the far side of the clouds
The pavement of no bird: when it half-opens
Earth is at the bottom of a leakage which overflows
The sun there descends green ladders
Lichen they drift in mid-air fogs
A shoal of magpies against a background of stems
Where polished houses repose

8 a.m.
When the tree fanned reveers
Like the branches of a tiger
   In every sense riveted

Revire éventé l'arbre quand
Du tigre les branches comme
Sens dérivent

10 h.   Au point qu'implique le poème
Mire je t'attends partout
—quand je prends soin de mon amour
Il se moque de moi—

Les hortensias préfèrent la maison
—Je lui décris la vie avec exactitude—
Les arbres autour imitent le grenier
La sève est la taupe du ciel

Rotule d'arbre et du reflet
Ici s'amincit la vie faite
De nuage de sable d'eau
Un couloir brille où l'aquarelle
Suffit à porter le bateau Ici

Galerie comme une main s'achève
Ou quelque extrémité d'encre trace
De gauche à droite ici
Condensé, alcôve, le signe de la terre

Ressource du mariage
C'est le visible
Aveuglément choisi

12 h.   Rouleau confiè muet qui pose
Comme peigne sur la joue le hibou le genou
Sur l'échine l'oiseau le portement de Siméon
Sur le style la tête de bouddha sur son ventre
Sur le pliant de ses jambes sur la natte sur
La terre le tertre des crânes et des pierres au
Début du voyage et les yeux de crapaud sur
L'obèse crapaud sur les feuilles sur l'eau dormante

Reveers fanned the tree when
Of a tiger the branches like
Senses adrift

10 a.m.   To the point where the poem implicates
Aim I await you everywhere
—when I take good care of my love
it makes fun of me—

The hydrangeas prefer the house
—For her I describe life with exactitude—
The surrounding trees imitate the attic
The sap is the mole of the sky

Knee joint of tree and its reflection
Here life made of cloud
Of sand of water thins
A passage glistens where the water color
Suffices to carry the boat Here

A gallery like a hand ends
Or some ink extremity traces
From left to right here
Condensed, alcove, the sign of the earth

Resource of marriage
It is the visible
Blindly chosen

Noon.   Field-roller entrusted and mute which poses
Like a comb on the cheek the owl the knee
On the backbone the bird the carriage of Simeon
On the style the Buddha head on his stomach
On the folding of legs on the mat on
The earth the pile of skulls and stones at
The beginning of the journey and the eyes of the toad on
The fat toad on the leaves on the sleeping water

Sur la vase sur la terre la pyramide et le caillou
Sur le grès sur le sol

17 h.

Le stock énorme que le fléau petit du millésime
Sur l'aire lavée de la cuisine écosse
La mer entre les lignes brille
(L'exagération du vent, le plan tourmenté)
Bergerie là-bas l'horizon
Lézard et l'urine des poissons font le bord
La maison qui résiste au soleil
La face des choses eût été changée

20 h

Hêtre ou tremble au souffle de femme embrassée
Un de ces jours où le vent travaille dans le bleu
Levant à sec toute chose comme un gérant
Et de toute chose secoue les espèces intentionnelles

Brouillard bleu de la philotês
Où la poreuse lune s'engorge
Arbres dont on ne peut médire
Et le tilleul raffole du tilleul

On the ooze on the earth the pyramid and the pebble
        On the quartz on the soil

5 p.m.
        The huge stock that the tiny beam of the coin's date
            On the washed area of the kitchen shells
                The sea between the lines shines
        (The exaggeration of the wind, the tortured plane)
                Sheepfold below the horizon
            A lizard and fish urine make the edge
                The house which resists the sun
            The face of things could have been changed

8 p.m.
        Beech or aspen in the breath of a woman embraced
        One of these days when the wind works in the blue
            Drily raising everything like a manager
        And shakes from everything the intentional species

                Blue fog of the philotheist
                Where the porous moon congests
                Trees which no one can slander
                And the linden is wild about the linden

Histoires des rechutes

Agendum

> Un merle arrête la circulation
> Une palme ratisse le ciel
> Une moustache comme une femme s'affine
> Ces jours sont en danger

Tout coule

> Le temps brille à cette arête d'eau ce por-
> Tement-eau de l'eau le long duquel elle
> Plie cette tige lumière qui n'est qu'amitié
> Du soleil et des yeux qui n'existent pas
> Mais acolytes au cirque qui tendent le rai
> Funambule où saute la meute d'eau

L'histoire

> Quand le monde était méditerranéen
> Que la nuit était nuit pour le monde
> Passer minuit c'était le seuil ni de ce jour
> Ni d'autre mais franchise dans un troisième
>
> L'histoire est devenue ronde comme la terre
> Et l'heure un projecteur qui fouille nos fuseaux
> Une ruse avancée leur jour espionne notre nuit

Mais déjà

Déjà
Dès la première repartie
Nous sommes en train de repartir

                                    A peine nous
Entrevoyons-nous
Depuis cinq ans
                la porte le visage (entre) bâillé à

Histories of Relapses

Agendum

> A blackbird stops the traffic
> A palm tree rakes the sky
> A moustache like a woman grows more refined
> These days are in danger

Everything flows

> Time shines at this water edge this wa-
> Ter-portage of the water along which it
> Bends this luminous stalk which is only friendship
> Of the sun and eyes which do not exist
> But are circus acolytes who stretch the funambulist
> Ray where the water pack leaps

The history

> When the world was Mediterranean
> While the night was night for the world
> To pass midnight that was the threshold neither of this day
> Nor of another but a franchise in a third
>
> History has become round like the earth
> The hour a projector searching out our time zones
> An advanced ruse their day spies upon our night

But already

Already
Upon the first repartee
We are departing again
                              We have hardly
Glimpsed each other
For five years
                    the door the face (half)agape

Les lèvres les yeux réentr'ouverts
                    Que déjà
Nous glissons déjà
Le train repart déjà caresse puis gifle
                         L'ensemble glisse
Démarre
          Déjà nous repartons nous sommes demain déjà
Ici dans le bureau
                    Silencieux dès la première règlique
                    Déserts dès l'embras
Nul visage nul échange ils redescendent un hiver écoulé
                    L'hiver futur

Pause

          Les mâts sur l'aire de lancement
          Seront encore ces frênes où le soleil
          Bat monnaie de vernal aloi
          Allons gaieté Ne pleure pas
          L'insolation du champ pèle en coquelicots
          C'est la terre avec ses revirements indépendants
          Et son mouchoir de danse qui fait encore la loi:

Haïku du visible

          Un   L'équidistant Lui le lucide
          L'impartial quand la terre dormeuse
          Se retourne vers lui

          Deux   La coque azur
          Incrustée d'arbres sous la ligne de pendaison
          L'air qui cède à l'oiseau
          Qui s'efface

          Trois   Le treillis le réseau le tamis
          Le nid d'intervalles
          Un feu de paille aussi longtemps que le soleil
          Et ces murs une piste de plantigrades

134   HISTOIRES DES RECHUTES

again
The lips the eyes half-reopened
Than already
We are sliding already
The train departs again already a caress then whap
The whole slides
Starts off
Already we are departing again we are tomorrow already
Here in the office
Silent from the first reply
Deserted upon the embrae
No face no exchange they redescend a slipped-away winter
The future winter

Pause

The masts on the launching pad
Will still be these ash trees where the sun
Mints coins of vernal sterling
Come on gaiety Don't cry
The solar heat of the field peels off into red poppies
It is the earth with its independent sudden reversals
And its flamenco-kerchief that still makes the law:

Haiku of the visible

OneThe equidistant The Lucid One
The impartial when the slumbering earth
Turns again toward him

TwoThe azure hull
Encrusted with trees under the hanging-line
The air which yields to a bird
Which vanishes

ThreeThe trellis the network the sifter
The nest of intervals
A straw fire for as long as the sun
And these walls a plantigrade trail

HISTORIES OF RELAPSES135

Murs tracés à coups de griffe
Et debout comme un moulage de combat

Quatre   L'eau bien épaisse bien ajointée
L'eau remplie remplissant
L'eau sans jour sur le poisson mouillé

Et la terre comme fonds la recouverte la patiente
          L'implicite

L'inscription

AUBORDETSURFONDDEVISCÈREINVISIBLE
MONTANTDEDOSVERSUNEFACEQU'ILCONNAÎT
DÉPOSSÉDÉECOMMEBEAUTÉDEL'AUTRE
ILPASSEDECHAROGNEÀROSE
PARLERITEFARDÉDELAMÉTAMORPHOSE

A nouveau

Le souvenir de robe qu'on s'était mise
Je vous passe la description   Demain
Comme une robe qu'on n'ose pas mettre
De sacrement de noce de baptême
Elle est pliée sous le noir dans le lit
Comme tenues de Bajazet à Istanbul
. . .
Le beau jour comme une robe
Remise maintenant à la remise

Le départ

Qui est capable comme un rêve le croyait
Sur ce globe incliné de glisser à échelle réelle
Par Horn sur la nature grandeur nature?
Seul un doigt parcourt vingt mille
Kilomètres en une demi-seconde avec
Nostalgie sur la carte bleue   Je n'ai plus
Que la chambre des cartes des machines des échelles

Walls marked by claw swipes
And standing like a combat casting

Four   Water really thick really conjoined
Water filled filling
Water without an opening over the wet fish

And the earth as funds the recovered one the patient one
The implicit

The inscription

ATTHEEDGEANDONTHEBACKGROUNDOFINVISIBLEVISCERA
CLIMBINGFROMTHEBACKTOWARDAFACEHEKNOWS
DISPOSSESSEDASBEAUTYOFTHEOTHER
HEPASSESFROMCARRIONTOROSE
BYTHEDISGUISEDRITEOFTHEMETAMORPHOSIS

Again

The memory of a dress which one had put on
I won't describe it for you   Tomorrow
Like a dress which one doesn't dare put on
For a sacrament a wedding a baptism
It is folded under the black in the bed
Like the garb of Bajazet in Istanbul
. . .

The beautiful day like a dress
Shed now in the shed

The departure

Who is able as a dream thought possible
On this tilted globe to slip to a real scale
Around the Horn on life-sized nature?
Only a finger covering twenty thousand
Kilometers in a half-second with
Nostalgia on the blue map   For me there only
Remains the room for maps for machines for scales

J'emmène cette femme au sacrifice seuls
Sur le mont Thoronet avec le feu du pique-nique

(Mais quand la terre se redresse à flanc de lieu-dit rocailleuse
montrant de quoi elle est capable force dix force cent raz de séisme
figé aussi longtemps qu'on veut l'eau troglodyte comme une haleine
ni la mer ne peut en faire autant se recourbe et regagne le ciel)

Ce qui ne dépend
pas de nous

     C'est ce doit être la recontre flegmatique
Dans la lice balayée aucune trace d'humeur mais la croissance
     Des tapis la succession des vignes
L'étonnante sortie de coffret des prés en fin d'après-midi
     Aucun désir n'est exaucé
     Les choses d'ici font figure pour ici
     Elle dit Tu me persécutes
     Nous avons oublié ce que nous trahissons

Tabula rasa

O texte privé des choses comme des bruits car pour
Les cris il fut écrit: vous n'entrerez pas
Ce trille écoutez cela vous ne l'entendrez pas
Comme un mot le vestige émeut Il en est revenu
Comme un texte il a tout perdu lui
         Passé par la mort

Alors le peintre

La peinture n'est jamais réaliste puisqu'elle peint le NU:
     Plume du sexe fichée en terre
Aisselles Étoiles Pubis Étoiles Palmiers Étoiles
     Noires sur la nuit verte
Les hanches catalanes le fort menton de femmes
     Giration silencieuse des profils
     La captation des faces

I take this woman to the sacrifice alone
On Mount Thoronet with the fire of the picnic

(But when the earth rises upon the flank of the site rocky showing
what it can do force 10 force 100 seismic wave fixed as long as one
wants the troglodyte water like a breath nor the sea is able to do
as much curves and returns to the sky)

That which does not
depend upon us

    It is it should be the phlegmatic encounter
In the swept tilting field not a trace of anger but the growth
    Of carpets the succession of vineyards
The meadows' astonishing emergence from a coffer in late afternoon
    No desire is answered
    The things of here cut a figure for here
    She says You persecute me
    We have forgotten what we betray

Tabula rasa

O text deprived of things as well as noises for in regard to
The cries it was written: you will not enter
This trill listen to it you will not hear it
Like a work the vestige arouses It has come back from there
Like a text it has lost everything
           Passed through death

The painter then

Painting is never realistic since it paints the NUDE:
      Plume of sex driven in earth
Armpits Stars Pubis Stars Palmtrees Stars
      Black on the green night
Catalan hips the strong chins of women
      Silent gyre of profiles
      The captation of faces

Et le chat
                    à son échelle
Les dents et le sang du cheval
Le langue à langue des amants
Il tranche avec pinceau le nœud gordien laideur

(*La conversation continue*

          Parler de lui c'est médire
          Se découvrir est son masque
          A simplement décrire ses mœurs
          Vous êstes menacé de diffamation)

L'inscription

ILYASILONGTEMPSQUEVOUSÊTESMORT
QUEVOTRETOMBEVIDEESTAJOURÉE
QUEVOTRELANGUEMÊMEESTPRESQUEMORTE
ETQUEVOTREPOUSSIÈREAREJOINTLAPOUSSIÈRE

Que

          Que le vivant n'est pas moins mort
Que n'est pas à savoir ce qu'il en sait de sa propre vie
Que ce qui paraît comme un mort qui paraît
Son livre à la main témoin comme un mort au détour
Avec la table en pierre de sa question sous patte O
          Monde aux millions de vivants
          Pour un seul nom mort en vivant

Pour surseoir

          Les os rentrent dans leur lit   Ce qui se défait
          Je ne le lègue pas car ce n'était pas mien
          La différence s'accuse entre ce profil et celui
          Du David ce genou et celui d'Apollon
          Le coq chante pour la trentième fois
               Survivant au corps à ses eaux
               Le souffle et les yeux en réchappent

And the cat

                    in its scale
The teeth and the blood of the horse
The tongue to tongue of lovers
He cleaves with brush the gordian knot ugliness

(*The conversation continues*

        To speak of him is slander
        To expose oneself is his mask
        To simply describe his behavior
        One is threatened with libel)

The inscription

YOUHAVEBEENDEADFORSUCHALONGTIME
THATYOUREMPTYTOMBISPERFORATED
THATEVENYOURLANGUAGEISNEARLYDEAD
THATYOURDUSTHASREJOINEDTHEDUST

That

        That the living is not less dead
That not to know what he knows of his own life
That which appears like a deadman who appears
His book in hand witness like a deadman at the detour
With the stone tablet of his question under paw O
        World with millions of living
        For a single name dead while living

To grant a reprieve

        The bones return to their bed   That which undoes itself
        I do not bequeath because it was not mine
        The difference accentuates itself between this profile and that
        Of David this knee and that of Apollo
        The cock crows for the thirtieth time
          Surviving the body and its waters
          The breath and the eyes were saved

(Nature moignonnée, un silence impressionnant; les animaux—
oiseaux la plupart—qui ne jouent plus de rôle dans le culte, retour-
nent à l'état domestique. Les horloges ont encore du mouvement
pour quelque temps, et voici que des bruits autrefois secondaires
comme ceux de l'indispensable cuisine emplissent les êtres et font
le silence du lieu. Il prit des mots, les distribua, se disant desquels
ont-ils besoin: Soleil, Liberté, Saül, Mésange . . . Mais ils se détour-
naient aussitôt comme des chiens trompés par un geste de la main;
ils restaient sur leur faim.)

(Nature stump-ended, an impressive silence; animals—birds for the most part—who no longer play a role in the cult, return to their domestic state. The clocks still have some movement for a while, and here are sounds formerly secondary like those of the indispensable kitchen filling up the beings and they create the silence in the place. He took words, he distributed them, telling himself of which ones do they have need: Sun, Liberty, Saul, Titmouse. . . . But they turned away immediately like dogs deceived by a hand gesture; they remained with their hunger.)

de *Tombeau de Du Bellay*
from *At the Tomb of Du Bellay*

Qui Quoi

Il y a longtemps que tu n'existes pas
Visage quelquefois célèbre et suffisant
Comment je t'aime Je ne sais Depuis longtemps
Je t'aime avec indifférence Je t'aime à haine
Par omission par murmure par lâcheté
Avec obstination Contre toute vraisemblance
    Je t'aime en te perdant pour perdre
Ce moi qui refuse d'être des nôtres entraîné
De poupe (ce balcon chantourné sur le sel)
Ex-qui de dos traîné entre deux eaux
        Maintenant quoi
        Bouche punie
Bouche punie cœur arpentant l'orbite
Une question à tout frayant en vain le tiers

Who What

For a long time you have not existed
Face occasionally celebrated and sufficient
How I love you I don't know For a long time
I've been loving you indifferently I love you to hate
Through an omission through a murmur through cowardice
Obstinately Against all likelihood
      I love you in losing you in order to lose
This me who refuses to be one of us carried away
From the stern (this jig-sawed balcony over the salt)
Ex-who dragged by the back between surface and depth
        Now what
        Punished mouth
Punished mouth heart surveying the orbit
A question for all wearing the third thin in vain

Mouvement de monde . . .

Et comment va la vie qui n'est pas éternelle?
Il y eut la clarté Il y eut l'énigme
Puis ce fut

Il y eut l'énigme Il y eut la clarté
Etre   parut   cela
Il y eut l'énigme il y eut la clarté
Puis fut la terre au centre de la table

Qui sinon ce sera la force des faibles?

And how is life doing that is not eternal?
There was clarity There was enigma
Then this was

There was enigma There was clarity
To be   appeared   that
There was enigma There was clarity
Then was the earth at the center of the table

Who if not this will be the strength of the weak ones?

Coup de silence

Coup de silence
              la distance   détale
       Écho de sans bruit
                     le premier cri   rejoint la douleur décalée
              décapité lucide

       Le printemps dégorge un froid miocène
       Déjà   l'été courcit   le jour
               Et   le   retard   annonce
               Et   le   premier   succède

Blow of silence

Blow of silence
             distance   takes off
      Echo of the unsounded
              the first cry   joins the out of phase pain
          beheaded lucid

      Spring disgorges miocene cold
      Already   summer shortns   the day
                  And   the   lateness   announces
          And   the   first   follows

Le mur est massif, de pierre pleine, dur, fini; pourtant il suinte Le mur est lisse, neuf et vieux, durable, et pourtant il est lézardé, et par la faille sourd et glisse une goutte, une bête, une mousse Le mur accomplit son rôle, il borde, il bouche, il sépare, il dérobe, il obstrue, et pourtant est-ce à lui de le faire, il protège, il soutène l'insecte à 100%, il se lamente, il adosse la décision, il est compté jusqu'à l'os, il transperce les eaux, il vient de laisser passer la main qui inscrivait, il met mortel en tête

> Ici est tombé
> Ici a vécu
> Ici est mort
> Ici a passé

The wall is massive, of solid stone, hard, finished; yet it oozes
The wall is smooth, new and old, durable, and yet it is cracked,
and through the fault welling and sliding a drop, a beast, a moss
The wall performs its role, it borders, it blocks, it separates, it
conceals, it obstructs, and yet must it do it, it protects, it upholds
the insect 100%, it laments, it offers the decision backing, it is
reckoned to the bone, it pierces the waters, it has just allowed the
inscribing hand to pass through, it makes one mortal in one's mind

Here   fell
Here   lived
Here   died
Here passed

> *And*
> *and they die*
> *and you die*
> *and we die*
> *and she / he / it dies*
> *and you again*
> *and I die*

Ici souvent je suis un peu comme encore un
Peu et je vais pleurer à tout moment était-ce
Deux millions trois cent dix mil neuf cent trente-deux
Sept cent vingt quatre mil huit cent soixante-quatre
Il m'a semblé que soudain je faillis pleurer
Quand en finirons-nous avec

Ainsi parlant il se tendait vers son fils, le magnifique Hector Mais
l'enfant sur le sein de nourrice à belle ceinture / Se rejeta criant,
l'aspect de son père l'effraye, Il a peur du bronze et la crête en crins
de cheval / terrible au sommet du casque il la voit s'agiter / Éclatent
de rire son père sa noble mère / Aussitôt de sa tête il retirait son
casque, le magnifique Hector / Et il le posa sur terre complètement
brillant / Alors son fils il l'embrassa il le prit dans ses bras / Il dit
invoquant Zeus et les autres dieux /

Encore un instant Monsieur le bourreau
Il n'y en a plus que pour un instant
Encore un instant Monsieur le bourreau
Parce que ça brille, la scène, parce que
Ça monte aux yeux le jour ému en pleurs
En pleurs aux yeux qui vont quitter cela
Qui ne l'ont pas non plus connu avant

> Tout ce qu'il va falloir emporter
> L'offre se tient, ce dont on fut privé

And
and they die
and you die
and we die
and she/he/it dies
and you again
and I die

Here often I am a little like still a
Little and I could cry at any moment was it
Two million three hundred ten thousand nine hundred thirty-two
Seven hundred twenty-four thousand eight hundred sixty-four
It seemed to me that suddenly I was about to cry
When will we have done with

Speaking thusly he was stretching toward his son, magnificent
Hector But the child at the breast of the nurse with a beautiful
sash / Drew back crying, his father's looks terrify him, He is afraid
of bronze and the horsehair crest / terrible at the top of the helmet
he sees it move / His father his noble mother burst out laughing / At
once he took his helmet from his head, magnificent Hector / And
he placed it on the ground shining all over / Then his son he kissed
him he took him in his arms / He said invoking Zeus and the other
gods /

Just a moment more executioner
It will be over in an instant
Just a moment more executioner
Because it shines, the scene, because
It goes to the eyes the day moved to tears
To tears in the eyes that are going to leave all that
That were not even aware of it before

All that one will have to take away
The offer holds, what we were deprived of

Un dieu ramasse le monde à ses bras
Qu'il ne savait pas Il doit repartir

Comme	Si
De	Rien
N'	Était

A god gathers the world at his arms
That he did not know He must go back

     As   If
     There Were
     Nothing To It

de *Jumelages* suivi de *Made in USA*
from *Couplings* followed by *Made in USA*

Table des matières

De l'autre côté de l'arche qui passait l'an   le mur alunissait ta chambre   O tendre souef précieux corps l'odeur de rose animait ta statue   j'étais un collier de ton cou d'encens   mais anonyme pour toi toujours   puisque tu ne m'appelais pas

La faute en est à toi amour se j'ai trop haï joignant ma bouche à la tienne. J'ai reçu de tes lèvres une telle amertume / . . . / j'ai reçu de l'absence une telle liberté que mon corps faillit s'envoler. Fuis-moi donc si tu veux que nous vivions.

La lune emmurait cette chambre   Le noctaduc aux plus de 300 arches en finissait   Tu m'avais revêtu à ton col encensé (l'exemplaire de ces fameux seins micro-cosmiques)   O précieux corps qui tant est tendre et souef D'aucun nom tu n'osais m'appeler n'oseras   ton corps en était à l'odeur emprunté aux manuels Nous renoncions à faire connaissance   (Il te faut croître et que je diminue)

(. . . conaufragés, qui se hissent, c'était toi, ta main si voisine immense entre deux visages le matin aussi grande qu'un visage en pente sur la taie, s'allongent à bord du lit de fortune, de tendresse apocalyptique, comme deux condamnés co-jetés en chambre pour peu de nuits peut-être, microcelles salées mouvantes comme l'atome fuyant du quart du millionième d'écume de la crête qui roule le méridien, dis-moi   )

Le filtre osseux faisait au temps un passé dans le dos le temps ne passe pas mais passe   par une aile en *atus* une main en *urus* Plus d'hommes sur le ciel que dans les champs   le bruit des enfers est passé sur nos têtes   et le tort est monté jusqu'à la torture   Il est monté la vérité le tort éclate   croyaient être une espèce en voie d'apparition   Notre partage comment le partager Ils   Le fruit de nos enfers est médit

Table of Contents

On the other side of the arch which was passing over the year
the wall was lunarizing your bedroom   O tender suave precious
body the odor of a rose was animating your statue   I was a
necklace for your neck of incense   but anonymous for you al-
ways   since you were not calling me

The fault is yours love if I have hated too much joining my mouth
to yours. I have received such bitterness from your lips / . . . / I
have received such freedom from absence that my body nearly took
off. Flee from me then if you want us to live.

The moon was walling up this bedroom   The noctoduct with
more than 300 arches was ending   You had put me around your
incensed collar   (the copy of those famous microscopic breasts)
    O precious body which is so tender and suave You did not
dare will not dare to call me by any name   your body had attained
the odor borrowed from the manuals   We were renouncing
knowing each other   (You must grow and I diminish)

(. . . coshipwrecked, hauling themselves up, it was you, your
hand so close immense between two faces in the morning was as
big as a face sloping on the pilowcase, stretching themselves out at
the edge of the makeshift bed, of apocalyptic tenderness, like two
condemned co-flung into a bedroom for few nights perhaps, salted
microcells moving like the fleeing atom of a quarter millionth of
foam of the crest which rolls the meridian, tell me   )

The bony filter was making a past in the back of time time does
not pass but passes   through a wing in *atus* a hand in *urus*
More men on the sky than in the fields   the noise of hells has
passed over our heads   and the wrong has risen to the point of
torture   It has risen the truth the wrong bursts forth   believed
to be an appearing species   Our sharing how to share it They
The fruit of our hells is ill-spoken

(pour peu de nuits peut-être—le jour enfonce les rideaux—c'est
la mer houle des veines creux intersections d'épiderme friselis de
rides, mascarets tavelures, que pouvons-nous échanger dire qui serait
meilleur rien que cette compassion avide de se transfuser   dis-moi)

Qui tu étais je te dirai qui je fus
Je te reconnais tâtonne-moi nous étions vivants
Par ces jambes pareilles aux jambes des déesses
Que notre main mutile dans la nuit n'allant pas
Au-delà des malléoles ou du pubis le
Sacre d'un approchement de quai et de bateau
Ton front étroit que je comptai avec l'index et l'annulaire
Ton axe médullaire en creux vers les lombes comme
Synclinal érodé ou le doigté des vents sur la plage
Ou mouette par abstraction de la coupe ou
Et la bouche mythique entre les jambes virgiliennes
Vers où je descends pour te forcer à me suivre
Te remonter vers le jour en ne te quittant pas
Des yeux non pas même retourné vers toi
Mais fixé sur toi malgré toute défense

                    (yole mallarméenne ou trirème
servile: plongée à l'unisson en l'abîme, ahan du corps
ramassé qui propulse l'aviron, pause, concentration
qui replie les muscles et la rémige, silence, ahan . . .
—*ratis* mis pour *navis* «*en poésie*» . . .)

tu me cognais le front pour marquer ton désir
tu n'y aurais trouvé que le désir
    d'être à bord de ton lit

    Au pied de l'arc où l'an récidivait   souef et tendre corps
litigieux   la pierre satellenite emmurait un sisyphe tu m'avais dé-
vêtu à ton col insensé   leaving you I   o tendre etcetera surface
signifiante   je vais au derme plus érosé   (mascarets tavelures
pores   isolés cela)   où change l'échelle et porte l'accouche-
ment   (tu vis avec et tu marches pieds nus sur un parfait dallage)
    (tonte, clavette, un jour; orage, bière dans la grange, menstrues

(for few nights perhaps—the day plunges the curtains in—it is
the sea a swell of veins troughs epidermal intersections fripples of
wrinkles, tidal bores speckles, what can we exchange say who would
be better only this compassion avid to transfuse itself   tell me)

Who you were I will tell you who I was
I recognize you grope about me we were alive
With those legs similar to the legs of goddesses
That our hand mutilates in the night not going
Beyond the malleolus or the pubis the
Coronation of a nearing of quay and boat
Your narrow forehead that I was counting with fore and ring
    fingers
Your concave medullary axis toward your loins like
An eroded synclinal or the adroitness of wind on the beach
Or a sea gull by abstraction of the cup or
And the mythic mouth between the Virgilian legs
Toward where I descend in order to force you to follow me
To climb back up you toward daylight without taking
My eyes off you not even turned back toward you
But fixed on you in spite of all prohibition

                        (Mallarméan yawl or servile trieme:
plunged in union with the abyss, heave-ho of the coiled body which
propels the oar, pause, concentration which doubles up the muscles
and the remex, silence, heave-ho . . . —ratis used for navis "in
poetry" . . .)

you were striking my forehead to show your desire
you would have found there only the desire
    to be aboard your bed

At the foot of the arch where the year repeats the offense   suave
and tender litigious body   the satellenite stone was walling up a
sisyphus   you had undressed me at your senseless collar   te
quittant je   oh tender etcetera significant surface   I go to the
derma more erosed   (tidal bores speckles pores   isolated
that)   where the ladder changes and carries the childbirth

repiquées; claies, un jour, meules désarrimées; marché, cercueil,
lierre, couperose, une vie; carence des pasteurs, ruts, méfaits et
mouchoirs, crachats conjugaux, dans un an; housses ferlées, dé-
suétude immortelle, un jour encore; trahison, couches, mésalliance
du voisinage, luxe, dîme du vent, amer amour qui tourne laid, droit
commun, hurlevent, sorts bibliques; stèles, perds, sillage, abus, nul
ne sait, je n'irai pas si tu gardes ton regard)

    poème anadyomène innocent comme tant d'autres qui croyais
prononcer la différence entre l'autrefois et ton commencement
(de plus belle il reprit de plus belle je n'en connais pas)   tu répétais
il n'y a rien à faire rien à faire rien   maintenant marque tes linges
repliés:

    La Tanzanie, les mégatonnes et le lave-vaisselle, le valium et
l'Urundi, l'ADN et le cok' n'existaient pas du temps de nos enfances
Ni les objets qui s'existentifient

ONULFNMLFUTA
OFLPSDECOCDE
IRAFLQUNESCO
SALTIBMRASKGB
QI

        dans l'   abilité du forum, s'amenuisa   (lapsus, faux
témoignages).   veloppés de ponchos,   pareillait pour satelle-
nite.   itéra   les mains occupées   velles parvinrent. Et la
pensée basse   yait genoux   Refaut la fiction [J'iltutelle
eunounous vousseux]   détresses   pologiques.
    différence amphisbène surmontant enjambant
le silence qu'elle produit

(you live with and you walk barefoot on a perfect flagstone floor)

(sheep-shearing, cotter pin, a day; storm, beer in the barn, transplanted menses; wattles, a day, unstowed hayricks; market, coffin, ivy, acne rosacea, a life; deficiency of shepherds, ruttings, misdeeds and handkerchiefs, conjugal spit, in a year; furled slip covers, immortal desuetude, one more day; betrayal, childbed, misalliance of the neighborhood, luxury, tithe of the wind, bitter love that turns ugly, common law, wuthering, Bibical fates; stelae, loses, wake, abuse, nobody knows, I will not go if you keep your look)

innocent Anadyomene poem like so many others you believed you were pronouncing the difference between the former days and your beginning   (worse than ever he started up again worse than ever I don't know any)   you were repeating there is nothing one can do nothing at all nothing   now mark your refolded linens: Tanzania, megatons and the dish-washer, valium and Urundi, DNA and "cok" did not exist at the time of our childhoods Nor the objects which existentified themselves

ONULFNMLFUTA
OFLPSDECOCDE
IRAFLQUNESCO
SALTIBMRASKGB
QI

      in the   ability of the forum, diminished   (a slip, false testimonies).   veloped in ponchos,   etting sail for satellenite.   iterated   the hands busy   ews arrived. And the base thought   yed knees   Remust the fiction [Iheyouyshe thewewe youuthem]   pological   distresses.

difference amphisbaena overcoming stepping over
the silence which it produces

Quand le monde confine l'éloigné à l'entour
. . . .

Quand le monde encourt un hiver
    de la neige que la neige, des bêtes
que la couleur butée, des hommes que les
fourrures noires: figurines marchant sur
les eaux et l'oiseau noir pas loin du centre fictif:
volant dans la pierre:
    aucun dans son élément
. . . .

Et quand le monde est fait
    —tout ce travail pour rentrer
un troupeau de teintes ocres vers l'étable
d'horizon vert noir de peinture
. . . .

    le minuscule et le spacieux
    s'allèlisent dans la toile

Et quand le monogramme de Babel
a introduit un récit formidable
. . . .

    Alors au centre du village, le silencieux
déchaînement de la tuerie, la giration du
meurtre, le temps occupé enfin au massacre
    Le foyer du sacrifice

(à Breughel)

When the world confines the remote to what surrounds
. . . .

When the world incurs a winter
    snow nothing but snow, animals
nothing but stubborn color, men nothing but
black furs: figurines walking on
water and the black bird not far from the fictive center:
flying in the rock
    none of them in their own element
. . . .

And when the world is done
    —all this work in order to round up
a herd of ochre tints for the stable
of painting's green black horizon
. . . .

       the miniscule and the spacious
       eachotherize on the canvas

And when the monogram of Babel
introduced a formidable tale
. . . .

       Then at the center of the village, the silent
unleashing of the killing, the gyre of
murder, at last time is occupied with massacre
       The hearth of sacrifice

                         (to Breughel)

Voix du paléontologue

J'apprends à mourir parmi les fossiles. La toile des vestiges devant les yeux maintenant moulés et debout comme un étendard: allées et venues d'il y a 800 000 ans. Je suis venu creuser ma fosse, mêler mes os, et déjà l'urine et l'ongle, le cheveu et l'excrément difficile à nommer, dans la poudre. Je suis venu accepter de mourir, étendre un drap funéraire sur la mort terriblement éloignée, filet pour remonter des millions d'années; je peux m'allonger ici; périr, et déjà morceler un corps, semer de poils et de fines écailles et de déjections mal aimées un énorme et paisible cimetière, moi le paléon. Je me fais fibrille, éclat, diamine, spatule, étamine, escarbille, je rentre dans le sol, moriturescent, parmi. Je rêve à *Purgatorius*, j'accepte, et non par démence qui fait un fracas pour disparaître, ou massacreur mental, mais je me suis fait humble, j'admire *Erectus, Habilis* . . .

et comme un cortège de mort des funérailles de campagne, (*Espoir, Zapata* . .) notre cohorte se répand, mort populaire, effective, foulée du testament de cendres, dépecée, se disperse, se dépiaute, s'ophélise

Je disperse mes cendres, la réssurection eut lieu de naissance, alors la vie ascétiquement est passage de cette deuxième vie, de René, combien de fois reprise, à une mort dernière où s'achève le cycle de métempsycoses, des avatars conduits à *cette* acceptation.

Voice of the Paleontologist

I learn how to die among the fossils. The canvas of vestiges before our eyes now molded and on end like a standard: the comings and goings of 800,000 years. I came here to dig my own pit, to mix my bones, and already my urine and nails, hair and the excrement difficult to name, with the powder. I have come to accept dying, to spread out a pall over terribly distant death, a net for hauling in millions of years; I can stretch out here; perish and already break a body into pieces, sow with hairs and fine scales and unloved dejecta an enormous peaceful cemetery, I the paleon. I make myself fibril, chip, diamine, spatula, stamen, smut, I go into the soil, moriturescent, among. I dream of *Purgatorius*, I accept, and not through insanity that makes a fracas in order to disappear, or as a mental massacrer, but I made myself humble, I admire *Erectus*, *Habilis* . . .

and like a cortege of death in one of those country funerals (*Espoir*, *Zapata* . .), our cohort spreads out, a common death, effective, trampled by the testament of ashes, flayed, it scatters, deskins, Opheliaizes

I scatter my ashes, the resurrection took place at birth, so life ascetically is a passage from this second life, of René, how many times recovered, to a last death where the cycle of metempsychoses, of avatars led to *this* acceptance, is completed.

Le fard

Il, elle, ne cesse de recomposer la face, de regagner la face qui fut perdue il y a un instant, et cette nuit, le fard qui comme les bandelettes de l'homme invisible ou l'appeau de graisses, le piège d'onguents, non pour capturer l'autre, l'autre que cet autre que je suis, décédé qui ne revient à soi que de comparer le souvenir de l'image récente au miroir et la supputation de l'effet de son image actuelle en les yeux de l'autre; le fard superficiel pour y faire monter, «prendre», se recomposer l'impossible aspect du disparu, évoquer l'incessant défunt qui se décompose, car chacun est celui qui vient de *perdre la face* en l'autre, et tente de réparer cette catastrophe: à l'instant, quand nous nous sommes rencontrés dans la porte et chacun recule d'horreur car il a vu l'absence de l'autre périr de trop près où il n'y avait plus de face, a vu le démembrement le morcellement de ton secret, là où on ne peut que faire l'amour ou le meurtre, démembrés, dispersés, écartelés, oublier l'unité . . .

Make-up

He, she, never stop recomposing his/her face, regaining the face lost a moment ago, and tonight, the make-up that like the mummy wrappings around the invisible man or the decoy-bird of fat, the ointment trap, not to capture the other, the other other than this other that I am, the deceased who comes back to life only through comparing the memory of the recent image in the mirror with the calculation of the effect of his actual image in the other's eyes; superficial make-up to make it raise there, "to set," to recompose the impossible aspect of the deceased, to evoke the incessant defunct one who decomposes, for everyone is the one who has just *lost face* in the other, and tries to repair that catastrophe: just now, when we have met in the doorway and each recoils in horror, having seen the absence of the other perish too close where there was no more face, having seen the dismemberment the parcelling out of your secret, there where one can only make love or commit murder, dismembered, dispersed, quartered, forget unity . . .

Oublier l'image

Je t'ai regardée comme le Christ, imaginons, Véronique et ils se départirent avec la face scalpée de l'autre
Leur *tu* ne date pas de ce poème conventionnel

Accosté à cette beauté si proche de toi, l'enseigne des cheveux battant l'autour comme dans une rue de naissance, les yeux me tuméfiaient

Le pansement des nuits va me drainer, je disperserai tes cendres; chasserai tes courbes, ta figure de «muse» inversée en cette jeune femme grillée qui cherchait la poésie chez des hommes, l'usurpant, ton âge de muse inverse ignorante réincarnée moins jeune à chaque âge
la charpie des nuits me guérit, ton visage s'assourdit, tes dents me brident moins chaque matin depuis ce matin

Et de quoi parlions-nous parmi des autres, dans la feinte générale que la beauté allait de soi, comme vaquait de soi parmi ce nous de feinte ta peau en beauté comme un travail

(Givre sur l'ossature finie, le front bis,
Le bandeau bleu des yeux à mi-visage,
Tempes versant et parois incunables sur
La bouche patente et les dents immortelles,
Trapèzes vers les seins peut-être, et le sexe reculé)

Demain soir s'éteint le mutisme de notre aparté, je ne porte plus les rouleaux de murmure cathare près de l'oreille

. . . de quoi parlions-nous feignant de ne pas fixer la beauté comme une espèce oblique que notre distraction mimée ne gênerait pas, ou parce que la beauté n'est plus, ou parce que la beauté doit apprendre un pied d'égalité, mais laissant à la dérobée le soin d'amasser la beauté de ton côté

To Forget the Image

I have looked at you as Christ, imagine, Veronica and they separated each with the scalped face of the other
Their *thou* does not date from this conventional poem

Moored to this beauty so close to you, the shopsign of hair banging around as if in a street of birth, my eyes tumified me

The bandage of nights will drain me, I will scatter your ashes; will shoo away your curves, your figure of an inverted "muse" in this found out young woman who was seeking poetry among the very men who usurp it, your age of an inverse ignorant muse reincarnated older in every age
the linen shreds of night heal me, your face dies away, your teeth bridle me less each morning since this morning

And what were we talking about among the others, everyone pretending that beauty was self-evident, like your skin looking very beautiful (like a piece of work) goes about itself among this pretensive we

    (Frost on the finished bone structure, your greyish-brown
      forehead,
    The blue headband of eyes at mid-face,
    Temples versant and walls incunabula over
    The patent mouth and the immortal teeth,
    Trapezoids toward the breasts perhaps, and the drawn back sex)

Tomorrow evening the muteness of our stage whisper dies out, I no longer wear the ringlets of Cathar murmur by my ears

. . . and of what were we speaking pretending not to fix beauty like an oblique species that our mimed distraction would not bother, or because there no longer is any beauty, or because beauty has to learn equal footing, but allowing stealth to take care of gathering beauty to your side

ton visage passer derrière le col, ton visage continuer derrière si peu de laine partout invisible, un millimètre de toile interdire ta peau qui remontait des poignets et des tibias se rejoindre aux versants sous la laine, se coller à toi

Et des hommes troublés t'invitaient mécaniquement, que ton oblique présentation ou toi-même sans fard comme une écorce énamouraient, maire ou président, parlant pour ne pas dire que tu tenais séance plus ouverte que par eux

Malgré le corps comme Casanova tu voulais savoir, apprendre, changer, mais les cheveux qu'une pesanteur à ton usage étalait sans relâche comme une source sur sa pierre, te trahissaient, et l'imagination démunie attrapait la plaie de ta figure endémique

Le tampon de nuit, je sais, va drainer les jeux injectés de toi, enfin je chercherai à me rappeler que tu fus sans jamais l'avoir été compagne bleue de gare à gare

L'étrange loi de ne pas aimer, que la timidité occulte de sa ressemblance, desserrera sa contrainte, et l'éclipse totale par ton image s'éclipsera en un poème

la dure loi de ne pas aimer quitte notre vasselage, migre dans le compartiment voisin, s'oublie en un poème

«je cherche mes mots»

allowing your face to pass behind your collar, your face to continue behind so little wool everywhere invisible, a millimeter of linen forbids your skin which goes up wrists and tibias again to rejoin versants under the wool, to stick to you

And troubled men mechanically invited you, whom your oblique presentation or yourself without make-up like a piece of bark enamored, mayor or president, speaking to not say that you were holding a meeting more open than one of theirs

In spite of the body like Casanova you wanted to know, to learn, to change, but your hair that a gravity in your service spread without respite like a spring across its stone, was betraying you, and the impoverished imagination was catching the wound of your endemic face

The tampon of night, I know, will drain the games injected with you, at last I will try to remind myself that you were without ever having been blue companion from station to station

The strange law to not love, that timidity occults with its likeness, will relax its constraint, and the eclipse total through your image will eclipse in a poem

the hard law to not love leaves our vassalage, migrates in the neighboring compartment, forgets itself in a poem

"I search for my words"

TO FORGET THE IMAGE   175

de *Donnant Donnant*
from *Given Giving*

Le ballade

En ce temps-là, façons de feinte et de tendresse, la peste ayant figure d'ennui dans les villes, c'était plusieurs abris, caches d'amour contre l'amour et de franchise contre le mal: aller parler, très peu, avec une femme apte à redisparaître, se mettre nus les visages, abaissant les mains, un téléphone suffisait, ou parfois sur un lit, échange d'autopsies, la nudité se faisait lente, grâce à l'autre, je demandais puis-je venir on ne s'aimera plus dans la ville occupée, sit tu es triste, c'était des entresols, recès d'insouci, plus mentaient les discours publics et privés plus montait le goût de vœux rompus dans une intimité de hasard, l'ennemi dans la place nous amenait à nous trahir, c'était aveux risqués aléatoires, et maintenant j'attends que le dégoût se relâche pour reprendre le stylo.

Paris

The Ballad

In those days, ways of feinting and of tenderness, the plague having the face of boredom in the cities, it was many shelters, caches of love against love and of candor against evil: to go speak, very little, with a woman apt to redisappear, to make one's faces naked, lowering hands, a phone was enough, or sometimes on a bed, an exchange of autopsies, the nakedness was slowing down, thanks to the other, I was asking can I come we won't love each other any more in the occupied city, if you're sad, it was mezzanines, carefree refuges, the more the public and private speeches lied the more the taste for broken vows rose up in a chance intimacy, the enemy on our own grounds led us to betray each other, these were risky uncertain confessions, and now I wait for disgust to let go in order to take up the pen again.

Paris

Étude avancée

A ton nom qui précède un nom que je ne connaissais pas
Ton nom commun sans nom propre à quelques-unes
(d'Anna Magnani neuve dentelée prête à l'Annonciation)
Et ta voix pour laquelle il faut chercher d'autres comparants

Avec ces traits grossis qui me rendent invisible
Avariés plus encore sous les loupes de la pluie
Je me hais jusque dans les chambres
Les guillotines lacérèrent la nuit

L'averse nous siamoisa tu disais
(Elle dit): la Grèce à Princeton
Une course sans vainqueur sur la piste aux pelouses
Nous attelait jusqu'à la gare où
La permission des yeux fut suspendue

            Amants qui vous aimez
Je ne connaissais pas le jeune héros de ta course
            là-bras   ici
        J'ai déjà oublié ce qui va commencer

Princeton

Advanced Study

To your name which precedes a name I did not know
Your name common without a proper name to a few women
(of Anna Magnani new scalloped ready for the Annunciation)
And your voice for which one must seek other comparings

With these enlarged features which make me invisible
Even more damaged under the magnifying glasses of the rain
I hate myself even as far as the bedrooms
The guillotines lacerated the night

The sudden shower siamesed us you were saying
(She said): Greece at Princeton
A race with no winner on the lawn track
Harnessed us as far as the station where
The eyes' furlough had been suspended

                    Lovers who love each other
I did not know the young hero of your race
                  over there   here
          I've already forgotten what is to begin

                                              Princeton

A la belle étoile N

Toast de Cassiopée même et Déneb en l'honneur de nos derniers feux! La terre en mantille de telstars joue à la roulette russe, une cassandre call-girl en concorde vers Caracas ou Qatar sable une coupe entre les salves d'Orion et du Bouvier, fines désintégrations de l'Idée çà et là, miettes en mousse de la Philia sur la nappe des latitudes et le faux plafond de voie laquée

C'est après le dernier jugement chaque soir quittant ce laps ensemble exaspéré, comment survivre à ce carnage de bègues dogmatismes—visage repoussant l'haleine vertigineuse, le visage plus masqué que le masque, qui nous contraint à nous passer les uns des autres—et que le paradis ne soit pas ajourné mais enfer et purgatoire et lui en même temps, le temps, et nous ressusciterions ensemble plus vieux que notre haine, nous donnant un baiser de Judas baiser de paix baiser

L'insomnie déchire le sac Décembre, saque la couette de laine noire où nous pensions dormir ensemble roulés dans un lit de mille milles, chant de belle haine où les trente deniers tintent, avec la cuillère de Régulus contre la lie, l'éclat des normes qui volent sous l'écume de la Lyre au zénith!

S'il sursaute au bruit de la fourchette qui tombe à côté comme Satan «depuis quatre mille ans», vaisselle interstellaire dans le monde calme, c'est qu'un rien, que rien, confirme à l'angoisse son attente des signaux

8 heures retourne la couenne nocturne; écorché de lisière, viscères de sillons, de poteaux, vidés par l'aine horizon précautionneusement, quartier gris reparaît au temple du carreau

Los Angeles-Hauterive

Sleeping Under the Star "N"

A toast by Cassiopeia herself and Deneb in honor of our last twinklings! The earth in a mantilla of telstars plays Russian roulette, a "call-girl" cassandra on a Concord toward Caracas or Qatar drinks a glass of champagne between the salvos of Orion and Boötes, fine disintegration of the idea here and there, foaming crumbs of Philia on the tablecloth of latitudes and the false ceiling of the Silky Way

It is after the last judgment every evening leaving this lapse together exasperated, how survive this carnage of stuttering dogmatisms—a face pushing back the vertiginous breath, the face more masked than the mask, which forces us to do without each other—and let them not adjourn paradise but hell purgatory and paradise at the same time, time, and we would resuscitate ourselves together older than our hate, giving ourselves a Judas kiss a peace kiss a kiss

Insomnia tears the December sack, sacks the black wool feather bed where we thought we could sleep together rolled up in a bed of a thousand miles, a song of glorious hate where the thirty silver pieces jingle, with the spoon of Regulus against the dregs, the dazzle of norms which fly under the foam of Lyra to the zenith!

If he is startled by the noise of the fork which falls at his side like Satan "for four thousand years," interstellar crockery in the calm world, it is because a nothing, only nothing, confirms to his anguish his waiting for signals

8 o'clock turns over the nocturnal pork-rind; scraped from the forest's edge, viscera of furrows, of posts, emptied by the horizon groin precautiously, a grey neighborhood reappears in the temple of the windowpane

Los Angeles–Hauterive

Iaculatio tardiva

Et il ne suffirait pas que je dise à celles-ci
Fais comme si tu m'aimais Montre toi montre moi
Tes Dombes ton Rhin tes Seine ton Ombrie
Comme Ronsard faisait son chant de son chantage
Pour de l'argent le sein des seins
La toison de cendres le centre de la terre
Faute de toi les mots ne s'assembleraient pas
Fais ma croissance Sans tes pores le pli n'est jamais pris
Je ne peux même pas sans ton échine ton antenne
Dire le temps sans la clepsydre de ton sang

Comme nous disons *Allume la lumière*
Je leur dirais Donne de la mémoire
Avec tes lombes ton sein tes saignées tes combres
Il y a à voir aussi sur les paupières

Iaculatio Tardiva

And it would not suffice to tell these women
Act as if you loved me Show yourself show me
Your Dombes your Rhine your Seine your Umbria
Like Ronsard made his chant out of his chantage
For money the womb of wombs
The ashen fleece the center of the earth
For lack of you the words would not assemble
Make my growth Without your pores the habit is never acquired
I cannot even without your backbone your antenna
Tell the time without the clepsydra of your blood

As we say *Switch on the light*
I would tell them Give me memory
With your womb your loins your drainings your umbrage
There is also something to be seen on the eyelids

Air Poétique 166

Cela

que boucle le chignon de la mer sur Aphrodite, ou que déplie la double Koré du Louvre large comme deux femmes en une en train de se tourner, ce quelque chose qui n'est ni «personnel», ni «social» celé «en nous», mais, par aucune censure psychique ni politique, différemment

désir d'ouvrage re-suscité par les belles œuvres psychopompes aux livres, aux musées, que l'ouvroir de la nuit souvent nous délivre en le retenant, «imminence de révélation», à contre-monde où la figure comme Gygès ayant perdu le secret de l'anneau s'efforce de réapparaître,

Cela, «silence et immobilité de Douve», est confié à l'écriture poétique—à *jamais*

Encore Cela, encore

C'est la vieille Déméter méconnaissable au foyer brillant des hommes qui échoue à tremper en secret l'enfant dans un bain de braise

Mais sa visite eut lieu

Et souvent ici, à lui à toi ou à moi, pétrifié comme les nageoires aux mollets d'une Victoire grecque, vertige au bord du monde humide, il paraît désirable, non moins, de se taire

C'est à cela aussi que reconduit l'écriture: fuir à travers le réseau implacable qui relie les mots, les livres, les dates, le carnage des psychés, et les phrases, les consciences, les œuvres; redéboucher à l'embouchure du désert

Reprise

> Gygès invisible chacun
> Ayant perdu le secret de l'anneau
> S'efforce de réap
> Paraître par les dents

Poetic Air 166

That

which the chignon of the sea buckles on Aphrodite, or which the double Kore in the Louvre unfolds broad as two women in one while turning around, this something that is neither "personal" nor "social," concealed "inside us," but not by any psychic or political censorship, differently

desire for work re-vived by beautiful masterworks psycho-pomps to books, to museums, which the workroom of night often delivers to us while withholding it, "imminence of revelation," counter-world where the figure like Gyges having lost the secret of the ring strives to reappear,

That, "silence and immobility of Douve," is entrusted to poetic writing—*forever*

Again That, again

It is the old unrecognizable Demeter at the blazing hearth of men who fails to secretly dip the child into the bath of glowing embers

But her visit did occur

And often here, to him to you or to me, petrified like the fins on the calves of a Greek Victory, a vertigo at the edge of the humid world, it seems desirable, no less, to remain silent

It is to that also that writing leads back: to flee across the implacable network that links words, books, dates, the carnage of psyches, and the sentences, the consciences, the works; to redebouch into the embouchure of the desert

Reprise

> Gyges invisible everybody
> Having lost the secret of the ring
> Strives to reap
> Pear through the teeth

Désir

Cette loi mais folle mais loi: de proportion inverse entre ce qui est et le dire; plus tu as ce que tu as plus ton dire est de dire que ce que tu as est ce dont tu manques.

Je ne désire plus ce que tu m'envies, je désire si tu me donnes à désirer; j'ai désiré ceci, et désiré l'entraîner dans mon désir à interdire sa concurrence . . .

Désir

Si le désir est ce qui ferait quitter tout le reste pour le tout autre qui ne l'est que de n'être pas le reste qu'on préfère cependant (aîtres, puberté prompte des chandails, crampes du pin en juillet) il porte sur le suaire du langage où le saint recompose.

Pars pro toto? Mais plutôt *pars sine toto*, ce rien que nous avons en commun, toi mouchard ou marchand, magistrat, groom, rentier, ingénieur, despote tropical ou douanier patagon, nous qui n'échangeons rien sinon ce même non donné mais que le poème propose à notre méconnaissance—secret qui nous pousse à partager l'intimité avec n'importe (quoi).

Reprise

> Et la vieille Déméter méconnaissable
> Au foyer brillant de Céléos
> Échoue à tremper en secret l'enfant
> Dans un bain de braise

Desire

This law but crazy but law: of inverse proportion between what it is and the statement; the more you have what you have the more your statement is to state that what you have is what you lack.

I no longer desire what you envy me for, I desire if you leave me something to be desired; I have desired this, and desired to draw you into my desire to forbid its competition . . .

Desire

If desire is that which makes one leave all the rest for the utterly different which is so only in that it is not the rest that one prefers however (estrus, prompt puberty of sweaters, cramps of pines in July), it pertains to the shroud of the language where the saint recomposes.

Pars pro toto? But rather *pars sine toto*, this nothing that we have in common, you squealer or dealer, magistrate, bellboy, man of leisure, engineer, tropical despot or Patagonian customs officer, we who exchange nothing except this even not given that however the poem proposes to our lack of knowledge—a secret which stirs us to share intimacy with any (thing).

Reprise

> And the old recognizable Demeter
> At Celeus' blazing hearth
> Fails to secretly dip the child
> Into a bath of glowing embers